LOST BOY

A Memoir of Love, Loss, and
the Hardest Goodbye

By Susan Kelley

You will lose someone you can't live without,
and your heart will be badly broken,
and the bad news is that you never completely
get over the loss of your beloved.
But this is also the good news.
They live forever in your broken heart that doesn't seal
back up.
And you come through.
It's like having a broken leg that never heals perfectly—
that still hurts when the weather gets cold,
but you learn to dance with the limp.*

—Anne Lamott

In memory of Timothy
With love and profound sorrow

Rest in peace, my beautiful boy.

CONTENTS

... and she loved a boy very, very much—even more than she loved herself.

— Shel Silverstein, *The Giving Tree*

INTRODUCTION

There are no words for the moment your world shatters. When the phone call comes. When time stops. When the air leaves your lungs. How do you survive the unthinkable—the loss of your child? This is not the story I wanted to tell. But it is the one I must tell—because to survive the worst thing that can happen to a person, you have to speak it aloud. You have to follow the grief to its depths, and, somehow, find your way back. This is the story of my son Timothy, and the aching goodbye that began long before he took his life. It is the story of a mother's love, stretched to its limits, and of the grief that followed.

For years, I tried to lift Timothy out of his unhappiness. I studied his moods, lived inside his sorrows, and carried his pain as if it were my own. I tried to steer his thoughts toward gratitude, toward hope, toward healing. But healing cannot be given—it must be chosen. My son bore childhood wounds that shaped the way he saw himself and the world. He often chose the role of victim, and I—unable to let go of what I could not control—lived in constant fear. In that fear, we both made mistakes.

I have written seven nonfiction books, but this one undid me. Putting these words on the page was both agony and a kind of release. As I stumbled through the darkness, I reached for every lifeline I could find—books, voices, and communities who had walked this road before me. They helped me breathe when I thought I couldn't. They reminded me that grief may feel unbearably lonely, but it doesn't have to mean being alone. The lifelines that held me up are the ones I now offer to you.

The signs were there, even in childhood. Over the years, Timothy received several diagnoses but too often resisted help. Families who love someone with mental illness know this pain all too well. I saved many of his emails, and in these pages you will hear his voice alongside mine. Tim often felt unheard; here, I give him the space to speak. His words, scattered across years—sometimes on medication, sometimes not—show the unpredictable rhythm of his mind, the highs and the plunges. I have arranged them not strictly by time, but by theme, so that his struggles, frustrations, and moments of joy can be seen more clearly.

In the end, I had to face the hardest truth of all: Nothing I could have done would have made him stay. The decision was his. Knowing that does not ease the ache, but perhaps it can help others understand the silent wars that lead some to choose death over life.

If you have loved someone who was hurting—if you have stood by, helpless, as they slipped beyond your reach—you may recognize pieces of yourself in these pages. My hope is simple: that by sharing my son's story—and my own—you will know you are not alone. It is not your fault that you could not prevent it. I could not save my son. But by telling our story, I hope to offer comfort, soften the isolation, and perhaps, even save a life.

ONE

RUPTURE

JULY 24, 2024

Day 1

There is no greater rupture in the human heart than losing a child. It defies nature, no matter their age. My son was my twin soul—we shared the same sense of humor, the same values, the same unspoken understanding. With his death, part of me died too.

I keep circling back to the same tormenting questions: How did this happen? Could I have stopped it? I married a man whose mind was already a fragile landscape, and I had children with him. I own that choice. I own my naivety. In the shadow of my grief, it feels like my fault.

Day 10

It still seems unreal, as if I am trapped inside a dream that refuses to dissolve. Shock clings to me. I have no desire to leave the house; food has lost its taste, conversations seem meaningless. My son is gone—and with him, the delicate hope that one day he might find his way back to himself.

The author, Sarah Payne Stuart, once wrote, "You're only as happy as your least happy child." I have never encountered a truer sentence. Timothy carried so much unhappiness, and I carried the weight of it with him. I believed it was my duty to fix him, to mend what was broken. After all, I had brought him into this world—how could I not feel responsible for his suffering?

From the moment I first held him, I knew I had been made for motherhood. My love for him was immediate—fierce, unconditional, and everlasting. Fifteen months later, my cherished daughter arrived, my second blessing. Some called them "Irish twins," though technically they fell a few months short of the title. Still, they were close enough in age to feel like a pair. They grew together like companions, side by side through each new stage. My two greatest loves, arriving one after the other, filling my life with a kind of completeness I hadn't known was missing until they came.

Tim, older and more inquisitive, often led with cautious curiosity, yet it was his sister who instinctively became his protector. Even as a toddler, she seemed to sense his moods, stepping in with a gentle touch or a knowing look when he needed reassurance. I remember one afternoon when his father didn't show up for a scheduled visitation—Tim's face fell, and tears welled up, heavy with disappointment. She reached for his hand, and in her soft, earnest little voice, reassured him: It was okay, and it wasn't his fault. From the start, she was more self-assured than Tim, less intimidated by their father's erratic and sometimes irrational behavior, and her quiet confidence became a shield for both of them. Their bond was a delicate balance—he would charge ahead, hopeful and mischievous, while she followed closely, protective and steady, guiding him through a world that could feel uncertain and unsafe.

But their father... his darkness was there from the start. It began quietly—verbal jabs that came from nowhere, subtle criticisms when I spent time with people who loved me. He worked slowly, methodically, to sever my ties to friends and family. Then the pushing started. The shoving. Always followed by tears and apologies. We were twenty-five, too young and too blind. Some days I think there should be a license for parenthood, with an emotional exam before conception.

Now, I move through days like a ghost, my phone lighting up with messages of condolence. Kind words. Loving notes and joyful memories. I read each one carefully, and with every one, I cry again. People say crying is good—that it "gets the sad out." But the truth is, the sad doesn't leave.

When the news came, I was in Boston with my second husband for what was supposed to be the final week of a long-awaited vacation. That week became a nightmare—waves of grief crashing without warning, aftershocks shaking me from sleep. Thank God I was there, in the city that still felt a little like home, when the world fell away beneath my feet.

From a friend:

> "I imagine there is no greater, more primal pain than to lose a child. It is literally unnatural. I hope you find comfort in the knowledge that you were a fiercely loving mother—all the more challenging and important when you are the "sole" parent—and in the warm memories." --Patricia

TWO

REFLECTION

Bill, my husband of thirty-five years, and I had just returned home from Boston when the doorbell rang. A florist stood there, holding thirty-six long-stemmed peach-colored roses in a stunning fan display. Each bloom rested in its own water-filled container. Tears sprang to my eyes immediately—then panic. Thirty-six stems! Did I have enough vases? Was I supposed to trim them all? I felt utterly overwhelmed, almost absurdly so.

• • •

I left a toxic marriage with the mentally unstable father of my children in 1972, after five years of trying to rationalize, placate, and change myself to make him happy, with two young children in tow. I stopped taking things personally and gave up the impossible mission of fixing him. Inspired by the new era of women's independence and by feminist icons like Betty Friedan and Gloria Steinem, I realized I didn't have to accept this marriage as my fate. Leaving was less a choice than a necessity—a survival instinct to save myself and my children. We were fortunate to escape with our lives. He had recently threatened mine. Later, I learned that he had continued his pattern of emotional and physical abuse with other women and children and was eventually diagnosed with schizophrenia. Divorce had never been part of my plan. I came from a solid, fully committed Roman Catholic family with five brothers; I was the second oldest and the only girl.

As our small family tried to move forward, my children—only two and three—became my anchors. We clung to one another for strength. But their father was not done. He appeared unexpectedly—at schools, playgrounds, even our home—ignoring restraining orders. My children feared him as much as I did. Even after he moved from Boston to Miami, the distance couldn't undo the harm. We were free of him, but never free from fear.

I could survive. But I could not protect my innocent little ones from terror, nor erase the trauma left behind. Years later, the stories they carried began to surface. Tim, my son, returned from visits with his father bruised in ways I could never fully know. My daughter—now a pediatrician specializing in child abuse—explains that children still love and seek their parents, even when those parents cause them harm.

Eventually, Tim could no longer carry his pain in silence. My son never fully recovered—and now he is gone, leaving me in a world I did not choose, with no map for finding my way through it.

My mother always said, "What doesn't kill us makes us stronger." Perhaps Nietzsche said it first. Neither has been a reliable guide.

And then there was my own body. At seventy-five, I was diagnosed with Inclusion Body Myositis (IBM), an incurable autoimmune disease that slowly steals muscle strength and makes walking, even standing, increasingly difficult. I rely on a walker now, my mobility compromised after several falls. Doctors told me that otherwise I was perfectly healthy—but years of unrelenting stress likely triggered the disease. It was the stress I had carried through my son's struggles, the trauma of protecting my children, the years of constant vigilance and care.

Caring for my mother in her final years took its toll, but the deepest wounds came from my son. I always believed I would inherit my mother's strength. She lived alone until ninety-five, and I thought her resilience was mine, too. When she passed at ninety-nine—just one month before my own diagnosis—it felt almost cruelly symbolic. Her leaving and my illness arriving, back to back, as if life were delivering one last blow.

For years, Bill and I had built a refuge in Florence, Italy. He painted landscapes, I wrote, and together we lived in a rhythm that felt untouched by the world's troubles. The diagnosis—and the falls that soon followed—took that away. We could no longer return.

There is no cure for IBM. My hope rests in a clinical trial I now participate in at the Mayo Clinic in Jacksonville, Florida, combined with diligent exercise. I grasp this as my lifeline, the one thing that might slow the relentless progression. During intake, I am asked to define myself: Gender? Female. Gender at birth? Female. How do I identify now? I am a bereaved mother. That is my truth.

In the early days after Tim's death, even walking to dinner with Bill felt impossible. I gripped my walker as joggers, parents pushing strollers, and happy couples passed by. Their cheerfulness felt surreal. I wanted to scream, "Do you know my son is dead? You're walking along like everything's fine, but you have no idea this can happen." No one around us knew that we were denied information about my child's death.

"I'm not hungry," I said.

"We have to eat," Bill replied.

"You must be grateful for what you have," people advised. I am grateful—but I am also furious. I have lost my son.

In the wake of my diagnosis, I began exploring the connection between stress and autoimmune disease. A Harvard Medical School study of more than 100,000 people with stress-related disorders found they were significantly more likely to develop autoimmune conditions than their siblings or a large group of people without such disorders. The risk wasn't just a small difference—about nine per 1,000 patient-years versus six per 1,000—but it was a meaningful one, reflecting the profound impact stress can have on the body over time. Many of those affected went on to develop multiple autoimmune conditions. Reading this, I realized my own journey—from years of relentless caregiving and emotional strain—fit this pattern. Stress hadn't just been exhausting; it had left a tangible mark on my body, a reminder of the burdens I had carried for decades.

Dr. Gabor Maté, a retired physician, bestselling author of four books, and well-known speaker, is renowned for his knowledge of addiction, trauma, stress, and childhood development. Maté uncovered the hidden link between chronic stress, autoimmune diseases, and women's health. According to Maté, there is a huge gender disparity in autoimmune diseases, with women being disproportionately affected: 80 percent of sufferers are women.

The gender ratio in autoimmune disorders has shifted over time, with more women diagnosed, attributed to societal stressors and cultural expectations. Women absorb stress from family and work, which puts them at higher risk of autoimmune diseases. Women take on other people's stress while looking after the emotional needs of others, particularly family and children. Maté explains how societal roles, emotional burdens, and cultural expectations are silently impacting women's well-being. We suppress our anger in our quest to take care of other people. He explains how stress absorption affects our physical and mental health. This is what happened to me.

Day 12

Today is one of those days when the weight of it all presses down. I spiral endlessly, asking myself over and over, "What could I have done differently?" Why did Tim change? Why did he turn away from me, the one who had always been his champion? I tell myself to stop making "the list"—my daughter's phrase for that endless tally of everything I did for him: the schools, lessons, sports, therapy, vacations, summer camps, the help with a down payment on a home, even paying for his divorce. So many parents never go that far, yet children love them anyway. I tried to meet every need, every desire, believing love could bridge it all.

Tim's passion was the Civil War. As a preteen, he collected memorabilia with fervor. We visited Gettysburg together, hunted for bullet casings across the battlefield at dawn, and toured the museum until our feet ached. He joined the Civil War Round Table of Greater Boston—the only child among a room full of older veterans—attending

Friday night meetings at the State House on Beacon Street and debating with intensity. How could I have thought I could mend his inner world, make him truly happy? Pep talks failed. Love failed. Support failed. I circle endlessly through "would've, could've, should've." The one immutable truth remains: I had a child with a man I should never have married. Everything else was beyond my reach.

Tim's despair appeared early. When things didn't go his way, he would crumble, and I saw it. I tried to fix it—with love, conversation, the best schools, therapy. I took him to child psychiatrists, but no one could offer a clear diagnosis, no one could explain why his heart carried such weight.

December 4, 2005
Dear Mom, I am writing from a hotel in Rockland Mass. You were right about Anne. She has serious mental problems. Anyway, she's thrown me out of the house. Another nice thing is that her mother called the police on me (second time in two years). It's probably too late to say sorry. Anne said that I had to choose between her and the children and keeping in touch with you. I did what I thought I had to do to stay with my kids. Or so I thought. Today, I spent my day trying to find a boarding house I could afford. Looks like my children will be

spending their holiday with a woman who wants me incarcerated and a grandfather who still smokes marijuana at age 65. I've made some really bad, bad choices in my life, but my god, could things have turned out any worse? It's been nothing but torture, rejection and heartache from day one. Tomorrow I'm going to try to sneak in the house and get my anti-depressants which, fortunately, is one of the few that you can OD on. I am sorry. This was supposed to be an explanation.

Love, Tim

Dec 4

Timothy

I am very sorry for the times you are having. But this can be sorted out with some clear thinking and planning. First of all, you do need to stay on your medication. If need be, go to the pharmacy or call them and order a refill. I can call them with my credit card. And please, Tim, no further talk of overdosing. Not sure I would advise sneaking into the house as that could cause further problems and upset with the children. It is very important to keep your job.

Why don't you let me know a cell number or phone where I can reach you and I will call you today. I am in Italy and the time difference is six hours later than the U.S. But if you tell me where you can be reached and a good time, I will call you and we can talk. Love, Mom

I contact my daughter— To protect her privacy, I'll refer to her as M.

Her response:

Hi Mom
I got your message this morning. Tim is hospitalized in Brookline at a psych hospital called Arbour/HRI (something like that) number is 617-566-8900/9361, number is permanently busy.
M: (Tim's sister)

Sent: Mon, 5 Dec 2005
Thank you for your help and intervention. You are a very good sister and always have been. It will take some time to see how this plays out, but I hope Tim is hospitalized for his own safety. The children are a big concern.
Love, Mom

Hi Mom,
I'm 99% sure DSS will not "take away" Tim's children. I don't think it is unreasonable that Tim is being told to stay away right now—they

don't seem to be a good fit (Tim and Anne) (understatement of the century). I don't know if Tim is sicker b/c that is the course of his illness, his family situation, or b/c of the stressors of being an adult and having to provide for a family, pay a mortgage, etc. One can only hope being told to stay away will make him pay attention to his own medical/mental health needs and make him stronger.....I also would be careful interpreting what Tim has to say right now, consider his source (Anne) and her motives, interpretation, etc.

From: SKelley
To: M
Sent: Tue, 6 Dec 2005 8:12 a.m.
Subject: talked to Tim

Hi M
I just got off the phone with Tim. He says the place is like The Cuckoo's Nest. Anyway, he did call work, he swore he was not on any drugs other than the prescribed medication. He went on and on about Anne, but I asked him what he wanted to do and how he saw the future. He does not know when he will get out and had to go to a meeting. In any case, he said DSS called and said he could not go home. He said he didn't know how they got involved, probably

the police. I told him I would help him to get a furnished rental for a short time till he figured out what he was going to do. I also reiterated that he should know more than anyone, how destructive it is to constantly fight in front of the children. He agreed. I will be interested in your take on the situation. Love, Mom

From Tuesday, December 13, 2005, one week and two days later, since the email from the hotel that he was going to overdose:

From: SKelley
To: M
Much has transpired. I spoke with the doctor and with Tim yesterday, Monday. He was being released from the hospital "Arbour" in Brookline, a psychiatric service for adults. He did not have a place to stay. I told him I was working on another place downtown but had no idea if it would work out. Tough doing this from Italy. He was being released, getting a cellphone with a prepaid card, and he would call me and give me the number. I gave him Christine the realtor's number to call about the apartment. He was going to Hingham, getting his clothes, and having dinner with the boys, he told me. He was planning on telling them that he would be living apart for a while. He hoped

Anne's parents were no longer at his house. I wait all day, my chest tight with worry, hoping to hear from him that all went well and he is okay. He has told me Anne probably threw out his clothes. I already have a backup plan: I will call Brooks Bros on State Street and buy him a gift certificate over the phone. He can go in and get clothes.

That night, I go to bed uneasy—no word from Tim. The next day drags by in silence and worry, and I begin to feel chest pains. I call and schedule an appointment with a cardiologist for Thursday at six, the earliest available.

Sunday, March 18, 2007 at 10:06 p.m.

Hi Mom,
Again, I am sorry. I've been terribly depressed lately. I did go down last weekend and stayed at a hotel, which worked out very well. The boys stayed with me overnight, and we got room service ice cream and played video games. They are so sweet, and so smart. It's been a very difficult time in general, and there is a biological basis that I cannot seem to overcome. I want you to know how much I do appreciate your support.
Love, Tim

Wed, Jun 17, at 4:26 p.m.

Hi Mom,
I'm glad we spoke today. Again, you went above and beyond in supporting me emotionally and financially these past couple of years. Also, I appreciate that this is not your battle to fight. However, I'm ready to take her on for sake of the boys. Do you know anyone who might know a reputable attorney in NJ? I don't have much dough, but I could do a consultation and then go proceed pro se. If you don't know, that's okay. I'll research.
Love, Tim

I reached out to a lawyer friend in Boston, who referred Tim to his brother, a divorce attorney. I agreed to pay for the divorce but set a limit, since the case was financially straightforward. I thought this would give Tim the fresh start he needed. Instead, he was furious. He said I had embarrassed him by placing restrictions on what I would cover.

But for me, it was about boundaries. I wanted him to know I believed in his ability to manage his own life. I was willing to step in during times of struggle, but I could not make rescuing him my lifelong role. The same applied with the car: I helped with the down payment, but the ongoing payments were his responsibility. My hope was that he would see this not as abandonment, but as encouragement to stand on his own.

> To: timothy
> From: skelley
> Date: Fri, 11 Dec 2009 5:01 p.m.
> Subject: The boys and Tim
> I have put $200 into each of the boy's Fidelity student accounts today for Christmas. My mother will send you a check. Please do NOT give it to your ex. All I hear about from my mother is the last check that was not cashed. It gives Anne power to tear up checks.
> Either buy a gift for yourself or the boys or send it to me and I will add it to the boy's student Fidelity accounts. Hope to talk over the weekend. Love, Mom
>
> From: Timothy
> Sent: Fri, Dec 11, 2009 10:30 p.m.
> Subject: RE: the boys
>
> Hi Mom,
> Thank you for depositing money for the boys. As to the check, I get it. I mean, I figured it out. Sure, took five months, but even this puree of withered dendrites and neurotransmitters that wreaks like six-week-old tapioca pudding finally has it DOWN. I mean, no more need to explain,

kimosabe, I GET IT. Not to NOT say "thanks for the 411" - thanks! -, but I assure you that it is locked in, tied down, tight as a drum, and never to escape. I have learned from my wicked ways/walked through the shadow of the valley of handing over checks, which is to state firmly and categorically and without any equivocation that I will not -NOT- ever hand over a check to the ex-missus. Cross my heart and hope to die. So, what else is cooking? Hmmm? Given that the great "check-giving-over" debacle/apocalypse still sears the heart, I'm thinking not much. Oh, me? Fucking awesome. Let's see: My uncle Jack dead a year, Nana dead four years, Aunt Ginny almost 9 -how time flies! - two children, separation, custody, divorce, four jobs, one suicide (incomplete), recovery from painkiller addiction, arrest for said addiction, four moves, shrinks! shrinks! shrinks!, one house lost and about a dozen girlfriends, each one crazier than the last. Wow. And not one -not one!- vacation. Been a little distracted is what I'm saying! Go freakin' figure! Maybe I should write a screenplay or something? Dang, and so I am, aren't I?! Flip the lid, kid, flip the freakin' lid. Love, Tim

Sat, Oct 23, 2010 at 12:43 p.m.

Hi Mom,

Hope all is well on your end. Things are really pretty difficult at the moment all around. Thankfully, the boys are doing very well and issues with Anne have appeared to have settled to a state of equilibrium that is tenable if not optimal. Work and health are another story, however, and it's difficult to try to pursue anything of a life when both of those key aspects continue to deteriorate. I feel like I apply myself as ardently and as diligently as anyone on this earth, but life just seems to get worse and worse. Sorry, but I don't know how else to put it. I should say that work is a major mind fuck on top of everything else. While said mind fuck might be alleviated to some degree were a better opportunity to present itself, I expect that the core issue would still be present, that being that in America in 2010 a 41-year-old paralegal is considered prima facia to be a disposable piece of toxic shit, pure and simple. Truly, the only way to fight my way out of this situation is to publish or sell a screenplay. I mean that literally (financially) as well as existentially. Everything else is zero sum. At this stage, time and health are arrayed against me.

So, if I can quote Marcellus Wallace from Pulp Fiction, "I'm pretty fuckin' far from okay." I don't expect you to understand, but I must assert here that I am right in the moral sense. And morality figures into the mind fuck prominently. To bring it back down to earth, the head of the department told my boss that I was joking around too much with some people. Now, I am without a doubt the most productive among my peers by any measure. And I know enough about human psychology to know that the person's goal was to inspire fear in me and to keep me in my place, a power play for her own aggrandizement. Fortunately, the department is a real gossip mill so I heard in advance of being told. The honest thing to do would be to point out the arbitrary nature of what was an utterly unfounded allegation. 'Course that would get me written up, so I have to take the low road and play up being a victim, basically get myself into a protected class recognized under the Americans with Disabilities Act (i.e. someone with a recognized anxiety disorder). Might get a few weeks 100% paid disability, which would be nice, as I might be able to finish up a couple of projects.

So, I am sorry for being a downer. I'm not likely going to be able to watch the movie, to delve into the past, until I've the present sorted out.

It really upsets me that I'm constantly faced by people who would insist on treating me as something less than human -- quite beyond the typical emasculating shit. On the flip side, for someone as mercurial and volatile by nature as yours truly, I've somehow managed to walk the straight and narrow despite an impossible amount of stress, psychological and physical. Love, Tim

• • •

Day 13

August 5: And then there would be a series of firsts. Today is my first birthday without my son. I am eighty-one. He should be alive—he was only fifty-five. The hope I once carried for his recovery has gone; at least his internal suffering has ended. His inherited mental health struggles began in his teens and continued into his twenties. Doctors tried talking therapy and medication for depression at first; when that didn't help, another clinician suggested Borderline Personality Disorder. I bought the book *I Hate You, Don't Leave Me* and read it over and over, highlighting passages. This was followed years later by a new diagnosis of PTSD resulting from trauma from his wounds and the pain he experienced due to a lack of healthy "fathering." It was the combination of the two that overwhelmed him. His then-wife suggested he was on the autism spectrum. In his forties a therapist thought he had ADHD and pre-scribed medication. He did not have ADHD.

Fri, Jun 24, 2010 at 6:08 p.m.

No shit, huh. My ADD medication is, well, an
amphetamine. When I get juiced up on coffee,
I barely feel my feet touching the ground. Love,
Tim

What torture it must have been for him—to feel
powerless over his own thoughts and the depression that
gripped him. Why was the right diagnosis so elusive? I
believed he was stable, at least until after his marriage,
when his anger and vitriol were suddenly directed at me.
He had tried so hard to be a good father, yet he was convinced he had failed. He feared he was becoming like his
own father. Perhaps he tried to cope through substance
abuse. And how many times did he walk to the edge, only
to step back? I will never know.

What I do know is that he threatened suicide more
than once. I remember one chilling moment—arriving in
Florence, opening my email, and finding a message that
read: *"This is goodbye. I can't take it anymore."*

The fear of losing him was constant. His sister and
I learned to respond immediately—calling the police to
check on him, praying they would arrive in time. At least
once, they placed him in the hospital against his will for a
24-hour psychiatric hold.

On Sun, Oct 24, 2010 7:00 a.m.

Tim
I was wondering if you were off all medications. I remember you telling me you had stopped everything. Your situation at work sounds bad. Are you actively looking for anything else? What do you do when you are finished with your screenplay? Is there a sales plan? Love, Mom
Sent: Sun, Oct 24, 2010 8:00 a.m.

Hi Mom,
I'm back on Ambien for insomnia and Ativan for anxiety as of a couple of weeks ago. I take Provigil most days to prevent somnolence. It›s the psychopaths I work for who should be medicated, though.
There are no jobs. I mean, financial services will never recover to where it was before. If I were younger and could afford to take a pay cut I would leave the industry. The embarrassment of being laid off my previous bank job has me really concerned about whether I can even approach those people for references, which only further complicates things.
I'd been deferring coming up with a sales plan as I thought it might distract me from the labor of writing. I have to think about it. Major

impediment has been health -- I have few productive hours outside of work at this point. Love, Tim

Sent: Sun, Oct 24, 2010 10:06 a.m.

Hi Mom,
I have symptoms that point to something like Addison's disease: incurable fatigue, diffuse pain, dizziness and nausea upon waking/ standing. Brain fog and disrupted sleep patterns. Incredibly low blood pressure (94/64). I›m sure that work-related stress and financial distress isn›t exactly helping, but there is a physiological basis, of that I am certain. I've come close to passing out at work on a number of occasions. I've been to the doctor many times over this. Love, Tim

On Sun, Oct 24, 2010 at 11:09 a.m.

Yes, I recall those symptoms you told me about before. Stress makes all things worse. Personal happiness makes all things better. (No, I won't print the tee shirt.) I wish that you would meet a wonderful, centered, emotionally stable woman and sell your screenplay for mega bucks. I'm lighting candles at the Dante Chapel and the Duomo. Love, Mom

Sun, Oct 24, 2010 at 11:21 a.m.

Hi Mom,
Thank you. I'm more grateful for your support than you can imagine. Love, Tim

Day 15

He knew it was genetic, yet he couldn't—and wouldn't—fix it. Part of him clung to the "victim" identity, refusing to release it or to embrace the possibility of becoming a survivor. When he married, I was no longer part of his world. He was an adult; the umbilical cord had been cut. I had no idea how severe his mental illness had become.

It's been exactly two weeks since that call. I stare at the clock—8:27 a.m.—the same moment the Weymouth police detective said the words I will never forget: "I'm sorry to inform you that your son is dead." He is gone. My heart wants to scream. My mind hunts for someone to blame. And yet my body, weakened by chronic disease, will not move. *How do you keep going after this?*

I replay our past. I was a good mother, a single parent doing my best. And yet, the self-pity creeps in. Anger follows. I feel hate for his ex-wife, who he said was unkind, who attacked his character. And then his final text—blaming me for raising him with no self-esteem, claiming that's why he married the woman who led him to this. I know it's not true. It's the illness speaking. And still…how can I not take it in? I am his mother. I must have failed him.

I don't want to face the world. This was never meant to be our journey—not his, not mine. Why me? It steals the little time I have left. Anger feels like self-sabotage. He had threatened so often. And now, he is gone.

Mon, Jul 25, 2011 at 7:41 a.m.

I've really lost all hope. I'm killing myself this weekend. Carbon monoxide poisoning. Please, no funeral, no service, just cremation and flush the ashes. Guess I will put in my last 4 day patrol here. Tim

I had just arrived in Florence when I received a disturbing email. His father had remarried—yet again—and somehow Tim had found the link online. He was very upset and needed to share it with me. He often called me *Tiny*, a nickname born from the fact that he was so much taller than I.

On Thu, Sep 15, 2011 at 11:07 p.m. timothy wrote:

Tiny,
Okay, my favorite writer is Franz Kafka. That being said, he couldn't have contrived

a story so twisted, so unreal as this: [Link to announcement of his father's wedding]
Of course, I'm not 100% sure. For the record, this is the first time I've searched in a couple of years—seriously. Guess I was a little bummed out about the reading, the absence of something akin to "Things are going to turn around in just a few weeks, just wait!" This is the icing on the cake of my day. Really. Love, Tim   p.s. hope you had a safe flight and settling in.

Thu, Sep 15, 2011 at 11:13 p.m.

Revision/Clarification:
I am sure (of course!!) Russian?! Really, dad? Russian?! (I suppose it's less cliché than Filipino, but not by much)
Thank God I have a twisted sense of humor and appreciation of the absurd
Samuel Beckett is a close second in terms of favorite writers
I'm not on crack cocaine, but this has me wondering -- maybe he was onto something? Clearly, I'm doing something wrong when it comes to affairs of the heart. Love, Tim

THREE

Rapture

My life truly began at Boston's Brigham & Women's Hospital on June 1, 1969. I can still summon the moment when I first held my son after an exhausting, thirteen-hour labor. He lay against my chest, skin to skin, and we both seemed to exhale into the relief of being together at last. It felt as though he hadn't wanted to leave me, clinging inside as long as he could. The doctors tugged and pulled, and finally, with the help of forceps at 3:10 a.m., he arrived—his eyes like slits, his tiny face swollen from the struggle.

The pediatrician came the next morning, peering down at him with a wry smile. "What happened here? Looks like he spent Saturday night at the fights." But I only saw perfection. He was my baby boy—the most beautiful human I had ever laid eyes on. Every milestone dissolved me — the tiny fingers, the first smile, the miracle of him. Even now, remembering, my face softens the way it did then.

Much of the past few weeks is a blur. Does it get easier with time? No. The loss sinks deep into your soul, and the grief of survivors lingers, relentless. There is probably nothing I could have done. It's over—forever—for him, for his sister, and for me. Was it suicide? Most likely, though I may never know for certain. All I know is that the pain does not fade. You learn to live with it, if you're lucky. But it hurts just as much.

Have I mentioned that my son did not speak to me for the last eleven years of his life? Eleven long years of silence stretching between us like a shadow. And then, only recently, he responded to my birthday text—an eruption of anger, frustrations, and truths he had never shared with anyone else. That brief, raw connection, after so many years, makes the loss feel even more unbearable.

There are no words for the anguish of a grieving mother. I wake with it each morning and carry it to bed each night. I could not fix his pain in life. I would not wish this on anyone. I do not want to speak to anyone. Nobody can truly understand the depth of the agony, the weight of the guilt.

His ex-wife wrote an obituary referring to herself as his "friend and ex-wife." Yet in that birthday message, he had poured out his anger at her, his struggles with at least one of their children, and above all, his love for his children. She will never know. I could not be that cruel.

And now I begin to piece together how to live with what has been lost, while holding close what remains: my daughter and her family, my loving and supportive husband, his family, and our many grandchildren who keep joy present in my life.

I know every parent believes their child is extraordinary, but Tim truly was. From the start, he seemed unusually bright, alert in a way that caught people's attention. While we were living in Cambridge, I even enrolled him in a Harvard cognitive study because he was so quick and responsive. At just three months old, he laughed and smiled with such maturity that the staff couldn't hide their fascination. I was just as enthralled—he was my first baby, and he filled my days with joy.

There were no signs then of the struggles that would come later. As a toddler, Tim was precocious and affectionate, covering me with soft, sweet-smelling kisses and telling me how much he loved me. Before his second birthday, he could already spell his name, proudly announcing to everyone: "I'm Tim. T-I-M. And I'm two. T-W-O." He also had an uncanny sense of humor, finding delight in things far beyond his years.

With my two babies tucked into a twin stroller, we often took one-mile walks to Harvard Square along Brattle Street with my friend and her son, stopping at Brigham's for ice cream along the way. On the return trip, we usually lingered at the playground before heading home.

At bedtime, with my babies snuggled in my lap, we listened to Chopin while I read them countless books. Those days were full of joy and laughter—motherhood felt like pure happiness. Tim especially delighted in the small wonders of our world. When the massive trash truck made its weekly rounds down Lakeview Avenue, where we lived in a spacious two-family home, he would shout with excitement, "Mom, the truck is coming! I need to put on my garbage man boots." He had a pair of tan, lace-up workman shoes from L.L. Bean, just like those worn by the neighborhood workmen, and he wore them with pride on these special occasions.

I exhale a deep, shuddering sob. I do not know how to get through this grief—it will always be there, this unbearable loss. My mind drifts back to Tim at age four: such a sweet little boy, full of excitement for Sesame Street, hockey, and his hero, Bobby Orr. "Mom, I'm gonna be Bobby Orr when I grow up," he would declare with unshakable confidence. By the time he was six, I had enrolled him in Cambridge youth hockey, hauling him to early morning games and practices, when the coach could secure ice time. Those mornings were long and chilly but filled with his joy and determination.

FOUR

REVIEW

For the past twenty years, before my diagnosis and the falls that made travel impossible, Bill and I spent three to six months each year in Florence, Italy, usually from September through December. Those months were ideal and productive—he painted in his separate studio while I wrote at home in our apartment. We had successful careers, wonderful friends, and a lifestyle that felt both rich and effortless. We dined out every evening and walked everywhere, savoring the casual rhythm of our days—until my health and mobility could no longer keep pace with stairs and cobblestone streets.

Since we could no longer maintain that routine, Bill suggested a new plan: renting a comfortable, furnished apartment in Boston's newly developed Seaport district for the month of July. He promised we could still walk (me with my walker) and enjoy the cool, clean air of the Atlantic. The apartment was perfect for my needs—no stairs, fully ADA compliant—and the modern Seaport offered all the accessibility we required.

We weren't in Boston often, but the summer heat in Sarasota, Florida—where we now lived—had become oppressive. Most of Bill's relatives, two of our daughters, and seven of our grandchildren were nearby, and we looked forward to long, happy days together. For the first three weeks, we walked a mile every morning. I felt stronger, with more energy, and we strolled to local restaurants for dinner each evening—sometimes alone, sometimes with family or friends. I believed I was receiving the real drug, not the placebo, in the double-blind clinical trial I had joined, and everything felt positive, hopeful.

That morning, I moved through my usual routine with quiet contentment: coffee brewed, a few moments of stillness, the house peaceful as Bill slept. Then, an e-mail pinged—a message that would change everything in an instant.

July 24, 2024 8:13 a.m.

Mrs. Susan Kelley,
My name is Bob Sullivan I am a detective with the Weymouth Police Department. Please contact me regarding your son Timothy Curtin. Respectfully, Det. Bob Sullivan

I stared at the screen in shock. Where had it come from? My stomach turned over, queasy with dread. I did not want to call—I did not want to know. I checked on Bill and heard the steady hum of his snoring, content and unaware.

I returned to my desk, took a deep breath, and let it out slowly. Then, with trembling hands, I punched in the numbers. Relief washed over me when it went to voice-mail. I identified myself and left my contact number. A little more time, a little more hope. Had he been in an accident? Was he in jail? I told myself I could handle it. How had this man gotten my email address? Grateful to be in Boston, close by if Tim needed me, I woke Bill: "Something terrible is happening, and I need you." Ten minutes later, the phone rang. I sat next to Bill on the bed, heart thumping. "I am sorry to inform you that your son is deceased." I think that is what the detective said, but I cannot be certain. An animal-like howl erupted from my body, a deep ache that tore through my core—so penetrating, so unbelievable. Shock overwhelmed me, and I began to shake uncontrollably.

What happened next could not have been predicted. Bill took the phone and, in his calm, steady manner, asked what had happened. "I'm sorry," came the reply, "I am un-able to share any information because you are not the next-of-kin." Bill explained that I was his mother. "His sons are next-of-kin, and they are in charge of the arrangements," the detective said. The rule was absolute. Tim's two sons—who, by order of their mother, I had not been allowed to contact—were now twenty-one and twenty-four years old.

Detective Bob spoke to Bill with quiet professional-ism, but every word landed like a weight in the room. He explained that the police had received a call from Tim's ex-wife requesting a wellness check. "He had a recent visit with his children that apparently did not go well. We had to break down the door, and we found him deceased. He was taken to the Boston Medical Examiner for an autopsy."

I sat frozen, unable to move or speak, feeling the room tilt around me. The detective's apology—he couldn't give us any more information—echoed through my mind. Every detail, every word, deepened the shock, the incomprehensible reality of what had just happened.

Bill called the medical examiner and spoke with a woman he managed to befriend, but even she could not give us any information. The situation, already unbearable, felt like it was tightening around us, suffocating and relentless. I was distraught.

Bill emailed Tim's now-remarried ex-wife with condolences, pleading, "How do we get to see Tim and say goodbye?" Her response offered little comfort: We would have to ask the boys, and she included their email addresses.

Finally, the oldest boy—my grandson, from whom I had been barred since he was about age seven—granted us a fifteen-minute "covered visit," just the two of us. He informed us that his father would not have wanted his mother to see his dead body. He added that we would not be invited to the sprinkling of Tim's ashes, which would take place later at what they called Tim's "happiest place" in Hingham. Every word was a dagger: I knew too well that he had not been happy there. The rules were absolute, the distance insurmountable, and the grief unbearable.

• • •

I had to calm myself enough to call my daughter—but what words would I use? Her brother's death would be shocking but not entirely unexpected. Siblings share a unique bond and a shared history, carrying each other's memories and experiences. The expectation to grow old together makes their loss particularly devastating, regardless of the nature of the relationship.

My daughter was a very kind and loyal sister. Tim was her only sibling, and she felt it her job to protect her brother from an early age because although she was the younger of the two, she was wise and nurturing beyond her years and often found herself in the role of mini-mom to her brother. But he had shut her out of his life years before.

When I called her, she was already at work. I so needed to hold her, to hug her. She couldn't come to Boston—she's a medical doctor with scheduled patients. She promised she would come to Sarasota later, when I held a "celebration of life" for Tim. I told her I would do something when I got home—perhaps a funeral Mass.

My daughter survived her father's abuse better than her brother, and is high functioning, but how could she not also be damaged by her childhood? She is happily married with two children, and they were about to leave on vacation the next day. Her priority, and rightly so, is her family. There was no reason for her to leave her professional appointments or postpone her vacation to join me. Except that I needed her. I cannot imagine what she was experiencing but it certainly had to be shattering.

She was called upon to save her brother on numerous occasions. When I was living part-time in Florence for twenty years and received despondent threats via email, it was M. I had to call because she knew the protocol and how to handle things like an intervention. She was a very good sister, and I was on a six- hour time difference.

No one in the family had heard from the biological father of my children in so many years that his absence had become a fact of life. We had neither the means nor the desire to inform him of something I could not help but feel he bore so much responsibility for.

• • •

As a mother, I watched my son struggle with depression, and it was terrifying. When he was deeply upset, he turned inward, directing his pain at himself rather than expressing it in ways that might lead to understanding or resolution. His anger and sadness often went unspoken, leaving those of us who loved him feeling helpless and desperate to reach him.

In high school, there were moments that shook me to my core. Decisions and events that seemed small to others could trigger intense despair in him, and we often found ourselves racing against time to keep him safe. He tried to hurt himself. On one occasion he swallowed a full bottle of aspirin, and we ended up having to take him to the hospital and having his stomach pumped. This was because his sister was offered a full scholarship to Choate, the high school he was attending, and they would be in the same grade. It had been his choice to redo his freshman year at Choate. He never mentioned it as an issue when she applied. This incident led to therapy for him and for our family, as we tried to understand his struggles and find ways to support him. No clear diagnosis emerged; he was simply angry and depressed, and he sometimes relied on medication to help manage the intensity of his feelings. Zoloft may have been prescribed then because at one point he was taking that. I was aware he had his issues, but we always talked it out and I felt we were getting a better understanding of how to address problems and disagreements. Here I was presented with "Sophie's Choice." I was so frightened by that episode that his sister did not go to the school. He always demanded priority. And we always caved.

Twenty years ago in Hingham, Mass., when he was married and lived with his wife and two small children, he made a second attempt, which occurred when I was in Boston to visit him and we had made plans for dinner with the family the following night. I was in a taxi on my way to get a haircut when Bill called and told me to return immediately to the hotel. My son had ingested a full bottle of Tylenol PM the previous night, and his three-year-old son had found him in the basement of their home. A nightmare situation was underway by the time we reached the South Shore Hospital. The receptionist told me I could not go into the room because it was "family only" and his parents were in there. I was his only parent. I barged past, nearly knocking over the poor woman, and found Tim in bed, packed in charcoal and hallucinating. The activated charcoal was part of an emergency treatment for a suspected overdose. His wife and her parents sat nearby, watching helplessly.

My daughter and husband, both physicians, had rushed to the scene from North Carolina, where they lived and worked, and through their medical connections arranged for Tim to be transferred to Massachusetts General Hospital in Boston and admitted to Blake 11—the Inpatient Psychiatric Service. The unit provides short-term, secure psychiatric care for adults requiring acute treatment, specializing in complex or difficult-to-treat conditions such as anxiety disorders, bipolar disorder, depression, personality disorders, schizophrenia spectrum disorders, and substance use disorders.

There was talk of a long-term commitment to McLean Hospital. I kept thinking, *McLean's is for crazy people.* The doctor looked at me and said quietly, "He just tried to kill himself—and very nearly succeeded."

Tim and I had many discussions following his second suicide attempt. A physician suggested electroconvulsive therapy (ECT) as a possible treatment for his inherited psychotic depression. ECT uses electric currents to induce a brief seizure in the brain, helping to alleviate symptoms of severe mental health conditions. Tim and his then-wife decided against it, concerned about potential short-term memory loss. No one asked for my opinion—and I knew it wouldn't have been welcome anyway.

A year passed after the suicide attempt, and all the worrying and obsessing did nothing to make him or me feel better. He couldn't cope, and he would periodically go off his medication and call me. There are unfortunate side effects to these antidepressants and antipsychotic drugs—depression and suicidal thoughts among them.

He would tell me he couldn't pay the electric bill or his heating bill. I would pay them. He made me swear I wouldn't' tell his wife. I said I wouldn't and then *he* would tell her. He would tell me he had no money. I would send him money. Then he would call and tell me his wife said I was laughing behind their back. *But why would she say this and why would he tell her?*

He'd been seeing therapists since he was three. His father often didn't show up for visitation, and Tim would sit crying and sucking his thumb. I'd tell him it wasn't his fault. His baby sister would hug him, whispering the same reassurance. One day, he told me he wanted to cut off his penis—and so I returned to yet another psychiatrist. We ended up at the Judge Baker Child Guidance Center in Boston (now the Baker Center for Children and Families), a place that helps children facing a wide range of mental health challenges. Tim had tantrums when things didn't go his way. The psychiatrist labeled it "acting out," and I can't help but think, in retrospect, that their guidance may have inadvertently encouraged it.

He grew frustrated with therapists as he got older. He told me one doctor had been dozing off during his session. But what did he really tell them? How much did these professionals truly care about my son? Why couldn't they fix him?

• • •

Tim's wife is mentally unstable and verbally abusive. She doesn't want me or his sister in the picture. She demands all control. She tells me he has told her awful stories about me and that he hates me. Then he calls and says he is sorry for what has happened. I tell him, "Just get well. Don't worry about anything else. You have two children."

I think things are going along okay. I get a call from him. "I can't make it," he says. I reassure him that he can, and I ask him if he wants me to fly up to Boston. "Yes," he says. So I do, and we talk and have lunch, and he looks like he is going to explode. His fists are clenched; he is grinding his teeth. Thank God he is back on the medication. He's ready to go look for a job now and he will then lose the government disability he's had since he lost his job after the suicide attempt.

I come home feeling marginally better, hoping he won't try it again. But he is in pain. There is no joy in his life. Words of encouragement fall on deaf ears. Then he gets a job offer. Good—he can immerse himself in work. The day before he starts, he calls to tell me that his wife said, "Your mother is going to try to take our children away." I assure him I would never do anything to hurt him—I am done raising children. And yet I can't help thinking: *Why would she add this stress when he is already anxious and insecure about starting a new job?*

But what do I do? I go to a psychologist and explain my situation. She tells me to stay away and says: "Of course his wife isn't normal; she wouldn't be with him if she was." I go back several times and tell her it is too hard to stay away. What if he tries to kill himself again? She tells me there is nothing I can do, and he may very well kill himself. I decide the psychologist doesn't understand because she is not a mother herself. How could she know how I feel? I don't go back.

My son calls me on Easter Sunday. I talk to his four-year-old and have a wonderful chat. He's so smart and reminds me so much of my son at that age. I say hello to the little one-year-old. I ask my son, does he want me to check in with him weekly? He says, "Yes, please."

A week goes by. I try calling him at work—no answer. Hours later, worried, I call his home. Still no answer, and no machine. I hang up. Seconds later, my phone rings—his wife, screaming and accusing me of hanging up on her. I take a deep breath and explain that no one answered, and if she happened to pick up just as I was hanging up, I'm truly sorry. She erupts with anger and accusations, claiming I constantly call and hang up. I calmly suggest she consider a phone with caller ID so she can see who's calling, if that's really happening. She tells me my son hates me and that I am the cause of his problems. I know I shouldn't engage, but I can't help myself—I gently suggest she seek professional help.

I plunge deeper and deeper into obsession. My son's struggles and fragile mental state consume me completely. My daughter doesn't want to listen, my husband grows weary of hearing it—but I can't stop. It dominates my thoughts, my conversations, my every waking moment. My body responds with its own rebellion: hives and angry patches of psoriasis erupt across my skin, my hair begins to fall out in clumps. There must be something I can do—something that will help him.

My husband tells me I have lost my spirit—and I know he's right. I can't write, and I've been neglecting the promotion of my latest relationship book. I feel like an imposter: advising others while failing to nurture my own relationship with my son. I feel the need to stay busy. How does sitting at home, consumed by worry, help him? The answer is painfully clear: he could call at any moment, needing me. I have to be ready to rush to his side, to attempt another rescue. He can't help himself, and I am utterly exhausted from trying to help him. Looking back, I realize how much we bent to his demands and needs—a dynamic that, in today's terms, would likely be called co-dependence.

• • •

I'm not sure Tim ever truly knew happiness, but I think he was closest to it at Trinity College in Dublin, Ireland. There, he had discovered a place where he felt he belonged, immersing himself fully in the academic and cultural life, as if he had finally found his rhythm in the world.

And now, in a haunting twist, he rests in an Irish funeral home in South Boston—less than two miles from where we are staying. After years of fascination with Irish culture and three formative years in Dublin, how could it be otherwise? It feels almost as if the universe has guided this path, giving me a chance, however small, for closure.

Our appointment was set for 1:30 p.m. the next day. My brother and his wife had just arrived from Seattle for a long-planned five-day visit, and their presence was a quiet reassurance amid the storm. Only Bill and I were allowed inside the funeral parlor, and the stillness of that space felt both surreal and painfully intimate.

FIVE

REALITY

We took an Uber to the funeral parlor. Clutching the note I had written for Tim, I longed to place it in his hand, to take a lock of his hair, to hold him, kiss him, and tell him—one last time—how profoundly I loved him.

When we were led into the small, dim, unremarkable room by the young male attendant, I tried to steady myself with slow, deep breaths. Bill gripped my arm with a quiet intensity, while I gripped my walker, blue veins bulging on the backs of my hands, both of us silently hoping I wouldn't collapse. My heart raced; I was shaking and unable to speak. A single electric candle flickered awkwardly, its light bouncing off the metal folding chairs lined up against the walls. My heart pounded, my body shook, and my voice had deserted me.

On the gurney lay a cardboard box, more than six feet long, covered with a pristine white sheet. Trembling,

I lifted the sheet, and there he was—my boy, hidden inside a corrugated carton, prepared for cremation. The box bore only his last name and a number, stark and impersonal. I reached to lift the lid, but Bill's gentle hand on mine stopped me. It was sealed, heavy, impenetrable.

We stood there, hand on box, breathing together. I whispered prayers and spoke to Tim in the silence of my heart, saying goodbye over and over. The grief was suffocating, a weight pressing down on my chest. I hadn't been able to ease his suffering in life, and now I could not perform the farewell my soul craved.

As we left, I pressed my note into the attendant's hands, asking him to place it with Tim. He nodded, and I allowed myself a fraction of solace in the thought that he would.

My daughter wanted to know if I was going to ask for some ashes. I don't want ashes. I wanted him to be happy—and better. I'll pack up all his diplomas, photos, and the lovely notes he sent me over the years, and perhaps send them to his "next of kin." The reminders of what was, and what might have been, are too painful.

I thought of *The Giving Tree*, one of his favorite childhood books, and realized—with great sadness—that I had become the tree, when nothing remained but a stump. It was shocking how similar our story was. The boy who took and took and it was never enough; the parent who could never say *no*. I had nothing left to give.

I just wanted to sit with him one more time, to hold his hand, and tell him everything would be okay. I can only pray that he is finally at peace.

SIX

REHASH

Day 29

I am grieving the loss of someone who, in many ways, left me long ago. I ask myself now: why did I spend so much energy chasing after someone who did not want me in his life? Where was my self-respect? The only answer I can find is that he was my son. Despite all evidence to the contrary, I held on to hope. I believed he would emerge from the darkness, recover, and find happiness and peace. Now, I am grieving not only his death, but also the loss of that hope.

And yet, here is Bill—celebrating the eighth anniversary of his second life. Eight years ago today, he leapt from a burning limousine on the way home from Tampa Airport. He survived, even while engulfed in flames, and against all odds, he fully recovered from his severe burns. Through it all, his spirit never faltered; his positivity remained unshaken.

These are the two men in my life: complete opposites—one consumed by despair, the other sustained by resilience.

My friend tells me I should talk to a grief counselor, but my situation is complicated. I think my son took his own life, but the medical examiner, who also could not give me any information because I am not considered "next-of-kin," said the toxicology report could take up to ninety days. Being estranged, left only with worry and without any understanding of the facts or circumstances, has added another layer of trauma and pain. For me, it has been a long, drawn-out goodbye—years of grieving in pieces, followed by the sudden, shattering shock of his death.

Can anyone truly stop another person from taking their own life? I still don't know. I am still trying to process this devastating loss. My mind runs endlessly—memories, questions, the relentless internal dialogue: *What could I have done?* The tears come without end.

• • •

I remember being stunned when Tim told me he was getting married. He had never really dated anyone seriously, except for the American girl he met during his junior year abroad at Trinity College in Dublin—one of his three roommates. Bill and I had visited him there and met them all, including the young woman who would later become his girlfriend. After Ireland, both she and Tim continued their studies in Washington, D.C., at separate schools, and their romance quietly carried on. Tim never spoke much about it, so when he suddenly broke the news, I wasn't even sure at first which of the two girls he meant.

He had just graduated, with no job and no money. He explained that he and his girlfriend planned to return to Ireland for graduate school and would work part time to support themselves. When I asked where he planned to live, that's when he dropped the real bombshell: they were getting married—and would find a place together. Everything had been arranged—without my knowledge—including her requested engagement ring. She had designed it herself: an oval diamond set in gold, down to the exact setting she had drawn. I couldn't believe it.

I felt a wave of conflicting emotions—surprise, worry, and a sense of being left out of an important chapter of my own son's life. Part of me wanted to be happy for him, to support his choices, but another part of me wondered if he was rushing into something he wasn't ready for. The suddenness of it all left me unsettled, as though I were watching his life veer in a direction I couldn't stop.

Determined to help, I went all out: I found the oval diamond, had the engagement ring crafted exactly as she had specified, and sent it via FedEx to Tim in Boston, just as he had requested. I was thrilled to see his temporary joy. They seemed to have so much in common, and for the first time, he appeared connected to someone. Tim had never let many people close; he didn't seem to have any good buddies. He asked Bill to be his best man.

The wedding was lovely. Bill gave a heartfelt speech, celebrating how they had met in Dublin, their shared interest in Irish history, and how they were friends first. I thought this was the pill that would make Tim happy. Finally, he had found it.

SEVEN

REMORSE

To hold a funeral—or not—was the question. I told my daughter I would arrange a Mass in Sarasota, Florida, once we returned home—no body, no ashes. In the meantime, I kept busy with phone calls to St. Martha's Church, eventually securing an available date. We weren't regular parishioners, only attending the occasional family funeral over the years.

I requested my favorite priest, Father Fausto, because he is kind and never judgmental. I also tried to find a funeral singer to perform "Danny Boy," perhaps with bagpipes or a violin. I had wanted the organist to play it at my mother's funeral, but she had self-righteously informed me that it wasn't liturgical. I was paying, and frankly, "Amazing Grace" didn't capture what I wanted. I called the priest, who intervened on my behalf, and finally the organist agreed to play "Danny Boy"—a minor victory in my long, complicated history of lapsed Catholicism.

But my daughter has a conflict and cannot come on the designated date. My friends here have been loving and caring, but most did not know my son. I moved here from Boston when I married Bill, and by then my children were already in college. I also do not want to explain my child, the estrangement, or his mental health struggles. I am sad, and I am exhausted. In the end, I cancel the Mass.

And then comes the predatory curiosity—the many questions: "What happened?" "Was he sick? The obituary said he had a long illness, did you know that? How did he die and what was the cause of death? Are you surprised? Did you see his children at the funeral? How did you find out?"

What do I say? I don't know, and that is the truth. I am not privy to the details, and there was no funeral that I am aware of. Close friends know I have had difficulty and he had issues and of the long estrangement between us. But who would understand the sorrow of a mother estranged from her adult child? Mothers tend to identify more than fathers with their job as a parent. The anguish of a child's rejection can feel existential, according to Rachel Glick, a psychotherapist and author, in a recent *New York Times* article. She says, "The phenomenon of adults cutting off their parents is on the rise." She suggests that parents who hope to reconcile with their children must learn to listen with empathy. Other people are shopping for gossip. I do not want to talk about it. The pain of loss resurfaces, along with my feelings of failure as a parent. I try to remind myself that I don't owe anyone an answer.

The Sunday paper arrived in the midst of my mental chaos, and like magic, there is this very helpful advice:

New York Times article from July 2024:

A Magic Phrase to Defeat Nosy Questions: Expert advice on how to navigate these questions.

First, "Take a moment to tune into yourself to see if you want to answer that question," says Adia Gooden, a clinical psychologist in Chicago. She explains that there are social norms around the idea that if somebody asks you a question, you must answer it. But you have the right to choose what you are going to share and with whom, "because often the answers are very personal." A helpful reminder is to tell yourself, Dr. Gooden adds, "I am not obligated to answer it."

Karthik Gunnia, a clinical assistant professor of applied psychology at NYU Steinhardt, offered his go-to response for invasive questions. In a calm, neutral tone, simply say, "I'd rather not talk about it." Dr. Gunnia likes this phrase because it can be used in many different settings, and it sets a limit "but feels less vulnerable than saying 'That's personal,' or 'I'm uncomfortable.'" He went on to say that it doesn't have to sound hostile or end the conversation and recommended following up with something like, "But I would like to share this story that happened recently." That way you're not rejecting the person, he said, just the topic. Dr. Gooden suggested saying firmly, "Thanks for your concern, I appreciate it. I'm doing just fine." If you decide to answer, do it on your own terms and be brief.

I have to learn to set healthy boundaries in order to take care of myself. I don't need to share details with everyone who asks about what happened, especially if I feel uncomfortable sharing. I will mentally prepare a short statement so that I can control the narrative. "It's just too painful for me to discuss this right now" or "I'd love to spend time with you discussing other things—that would be really helpful to me right now."

EIGHT

RECOMMENDATIONS

Fri, Jun 1, 2012 at 10:49 a.m.

Mom,
I don't expect you or anyone else to understand, but at this point I'm working for the weekend. My life - a life I wish had never come to pass - is more than half over, with the prospect of that which I have wanted more than anything else - the only thing, really, to be understood and valued - proving to be as elusive and unattainable as ever.

I feel that I was shit out into this world of inherited conflicts without much thought or regard. I mean, no one has ever taken me seriously. It took a long time for this to sink in, I mean, to really sink in. It took a long time to get beyond the pain of physical abuse and psychological torture at the hands of one parent and to come to terms with the full import of the raised eyebrows and guffaws of laughter my suffering as a child evoked from those putatively close to me -- the full import being that no one cares or has ever cared, really.

I'm not sure when it happened, but I did die some time ago. And that is the truth. I mean, I don't care/I give up - that's tantamount to death, right? In the past, I've made sincere attempts to listen to and to understand those close to me. But I don't think that anyone in my life has ever extended me the same courtesy, let alone the same compassion. In short, I don't feel heard. And I am done trying.

I have a few more years trying to be a dad, if you can call the farce I play into as away parenting. Then I'm dropping off the grid forever. Cashing out. If I can, I'm going to change my name. And not just my middle name. My whole name. I don't want to remember any of this.

And that's it. Tim

On Sun, Jun 10, 2012 at 12:48 p.m.

Dear Timothy,
Your points have been poignantly expressed. My hope and wish for you is that your life will be filled with happiness and love. It has always been my belief that you can overcome the

severe traumas you experienced as a child. You had no control over what happened to you; it must have been very frightening for you. Your father set out to torture me, you and your sister. It's over. It was terrible for all of us. I do understand. I am sorry if you think I contributed to it. But it's time to move on. The damage has been done. Your past contributed to your unhappiness but you can control what happens now. Don't let your past define you. You are a brilliant writer and natural wit and you are the father of two sons. You could turn your life around with your screenplays. I fervently believe that. I have always believed in you.

But, did other people care about you, did they understand you, did they believe in you? Absolutely. There's a long list of people who believed in you and we've gone through that catalog many times. Let's start with Bill, who you might want to take a moment to be grateful to-- my new husband, who we have never called a step- father and who has been so emotionally and financially supportive of you from day one. If he didn't believe in you, he wouldn't have helped with schools, trips, down payments for your house and money for your children. But the real key is believing in

yourself. No one can do that for you--but you.
It is your choice.

Your pain has become my pain and **I don't** have
a long life in front of me; this August I will be 69.
That means I am entering my 70th year. I hope
I have 10 healthy years after that. I hope you
and your children will come to my 70th birthday
celebration wherever that may be.

In the meantime, I hope you are well and feeling
better after your 43rd birthday. Love, Mom

With numerous threats of suicide and two previous attempts over the years, I knew there was a possibility he would
try again: There was always anticipatory grief. I had pre-
grieved, I worried so much; but when it finally happened it hit
me with vicious force. I wasn't prepared. There was no sense
of peace or relief, just savage pain and overwhelming loss.

It feels strange, living in a home surrounded by family
photos. Some days, when I look at a picture of my son, it
brings a smile; other times, the same image brings me to
tears. I can't seem to stop rehashing it all with Bill—every
detail, every possibility—tormenting myself with what I
might have done differently to prevent it.

Our mutual friend Paul, a retired psychoanalyst, rec-
ommends a book, and I in turn would highly recommend

it to others: *The Grieving Brain: The Surprising Science of How We Learn from Love and Loss.*

Mary-Frances O'Connor, Ph.D., studies those complex feelings for a living. She's the director of the Grief, Loss and Social Stress Lab at the University of Arizona. Among the many eye-opening insights you'll find in *The Grieving Brain is that there*'s an important difference between *grief* and *grieving.*

"Grief is that feeling that just knocks you off your feet—the wave of sadness that overtakes you," Dr. O'Connor explains. "Grieving, on the other hand, is the way that experience of grief changes over time, without ever going away." The key to that distinction is the part about changing through time. O'Connor says it's important to remember that "adjusting" to a loss doesn't mean you'll never feel that pang of sadness again—even decades later. But the process of grieving shows us that eventually we'll acquire the tools to navigate those difficult feelings without being completely paralyzed by them. "It's not just that 'time heals'—it's having experiences of what it means to live in the world as a parent whose child has died or a sister whose sister has died," she explains. "It takes a long time to really enable the brain to understand what things are like now. What does it mean for my life now that this person is no longer here? How should I behave in the future? What goals and plans do I make now that my life is so completely different?"

This from a good friend; I am not alone:

My sister also had mental health problems and it didn't help that she married a guy who turned out to be gay. She was devastated and killed herself while she was studying for her doctorate with him in Spain. You never get over these things but they begin to fade a little over time. You did the best you could and so did my family, but we just couldn't change the illness and the non-supportive totally self-absorbed husband.

My mother was a clinical psychologist and my sister had very good medical and psychiatric care. Her husband was a closet drinker as I discovered when he stayed with me a year before she died; I was sure he was clearly an alcoholic when after he left my apartment a week later I noticed every liquor (even stuff like triple sec) was gone. And then on top of that he came out as gay, which further unstabilized her. She had thyroid problems as well as manic depressive disorder and that plus the disastrous marriage did her in. You couldn't have changed it.

I know how it feels. And the constant worry about a phone call saying something has happened. You did all you could. No regrets. I am so sorry. Yes I know. People kept asking me how my sister died. I got so sick and upset with it I finally said to one nosy person that she had hung herself. That was true and it was the last time she asked. Manic depressive illness or whatever it is called now is terrible, especially if people don't take their meds.

If you have been through it you know how it hurts. No matter what you try to do nothing seems to work. It was like a constant ache always waiting for the next crisis which always came. But just imagine what it must be like for people with kids or sibs who kill or maim other people. Even worse. Get this; my sister's husband about 5 years later called my mother to get my sister's death certificate which he needed (had lost it) because he was in some scheme to fake marry a Siberian so she could get citizenship. I think he is dead now.

At least you have your daughter. And sooner or later a relationship with the grands.

NINE

RESISTANCE

How long must I carry this weight of complex emotions? I was not able to help my child. Will I ever feel peace or joy again? I am deeply saddened that we were never allowed to see our grandchildren—so much animosity. This is part of why I am sick. I need to choose joy over hate and blame. Back to the recumbent bike, back to healing. Falling apart is not going to bring him back. Healing does not mean forgetting; it means learning to coexist with the ache, to carry love and loss in the same heart.

I had my children—they were my life. I met my second and final husband after seventeen years as a single mother. I thought I had it all. And then Tim withdrew from us emotionally, becoming the focus of my attention to such an extent that, perhaps without realizing it, I pushed my other child away in my desperate attempts to understand.

God has a sense of humor. Today, as I struggled to walk with my walker to retrieve days' worth of neglected mail, I found an invitation for a free lunch at Tommy Bahama—provided I attend a lecture about cremation.

Something is missing. There is a hole in my heart. The milestones I will never witness—Tim's children's birthdays, graduations, weddings—have been stolen from me by his mental illness. The pain is acute. I don't know that it will ever fade. How do other people get through this?

My mother was a strong woman. After my father died, she carried on with remarkable resilience. I was distraught by his passing, but for me it felt like the natural order of things—he was eighty-four and had cancer. For her, though, it was different. My parents had been married for more than sixty years, inseparable, each other's confidant and best friend. Yet she didn't collapse into grief. She didn't go around crying or feeling sorry for herself.

Her faith took over and carried her through. She built a new life, formed new friendships, and spoke of my father often in everyday conversation. She might say, "Oh, your father would've loved that," but never in a way that suggested she thought he was still there or might return. There was no *magical thinking* for her.

I still don't fully understand how she managed that loss with such grace. She was strong, yes, but also deeply religious—a devout Roman Catholic, born in the Bronx. She lived nineteen more years after his death and passed away peacefully at ninety-nine years and one month.

But the loss of a child is different; children are not supposed to predecease their parents. In my case, the troubles with Timothy had been ongoing for many years. Not long after he had his first child, our communication slowed to a near halt. His wife wanted nothing to do with his family and drove a wedge between us. I think Tim tried to navigate it as best he could.

When my daughter was getting married, his wife was pregnant and said it was too close to her due date to travel from Boston to New York. Tim came alone. The following year, my daughter graduated from Columbia Medical School, and once again his wife refused to attend, claiming New York was unsafe for their one-year-old. I had even rented a car service with a professional driver and a baby car seat, hoping it would help. Tim still came alone. He was trying, in his own way, to be a good son and brother.

But he seemed unable to cope with the stress of his new roles as husband and father. He needed someone to blame—and I became the target. The disappointment and hurt built slowly, like a quiet, persistent ache. I held on to hope, believing it was temporary. That hope kept me going: the belief that somehow, miraculously, things would turn around; that he would realize he needed his family, that we loved him very much, and that we would do anything for him.

Yet each year, each missed milestone, each cold silence wore away at me. The grief accumulated in small, relentless increments, a weight I carried silently, hoping against reason that love and patience could bridge the divide.

While raising my children, I worked as a commercial photographic model. I appeared in countless ads—from *Brides* magazine to *Boston Magazine* covers, Jordan Marsh campaigns, and a variety of product advertisements and TV commercials. My agent, Maggie, often needed children for "family" ads and would say with a grin, "Use Susan's children—they're fucking gorgeous." Before long, my kids were swept up into the modeling world alongside me, and it became more than just work—it helped us regain our footing financially. Every paycheck they earned went straight into a bank account I set aside for their future schooling, a small act of security amid the whirlwind of our lives.

This went on for years. My children appeared in ads for everything from bank trust funds to Dunkin' Donuts, from toy boxes to countless other products. It became a familiar rhythm in our lives—a blend of work, family, and the small triumphs that helped us stay afloat. Then one day, Timothy turned to me and said, "You have to decide what you want me to be. I'm missing a Latin test today because of a modeling job, and I don't want to do this anymore." I was surprised; he had always seemed to enjoy it and was extraordinarily photogenic.

I called Maggie and put Tim on the phone. Standing beside him, I listened as he declared, "Maggie, I'm retiring." Maggie, astonished, couldn't hide her surprise: "What are you talking about? You're too young to retire!" But in that moment, I saw a quiet bravery in him—a decisive claim over his own life. That day marked the end of his modeling career, a chapter closed on his own terms.

Meanwhile, I moved toward my true passion: writing. I sold my first book, which propelled me forward with Tim and his sister as my biggest fans. They even attended my first book signing at Bloomingdale's in Chestnut Hill, along with Nana, their paternal grandmother. The book, *Real Women Send Flowers*, gave me a tremendous send-off, and my children, still in grammar school, were so proud of their mother. It remains one of my most cherished memories.

I need to hold onto these good memories and let them remind me of the joy and pride my children brought into my life.

TEN

RESILIENCE

Day 30

Today is August 22, 2024. I mention it only because twenty-two has always been my lucky number. I remember when I was a naïve, newly twenty-two-year-old stewardess—the term *flight attendant* wouldn't come into use for many years. I was in London with a coworker who knew someone who told us to check out a place called *The Pair of Shoes Club*—at least, I think that was the name. I was young, trim, and pretty, wearing a black-and-white tweed suit, as I recall. In those days, stewardesses were held in high regard—second only to movie stars. We had barely stepped inside when a woman gushed that she loved my suit and asked if it was Chanel. I had no idea what she was talking about. It was probably something I'd picked up at Loehmann's, the discount store known for its designer bargains.

It turned out to be an upscale gambling club, and everyone was drinking. We were supposed to meet my friend's acquaintance there, who arrived with a "friend." My date? I was traveling with the *jet set*, though I was certainly no jet setter.

The posh men were gambling, and one asked me to give him a lucky number. "Twenty-two," I said, smugly. He won big. He played it again—and won again. Chips began to pile up in front of him. Grinning, he scooped up a handful and handed them to me as some sort of commission, giving my friend the same. She immediately started shooting dice and lost every time.

After watching that waste, I decided to cash in my chips, valued at about 500 English pounds. I felt smart, lucky, and happy—and I've always considered 22 my lucky number since. With my winnings, I flew to Ireland a few days later, bought a Yorkshire terrier, and brought him home with me. Tara—my first dog.

Over the years, I returned to Ireland several times. In 1981, while my children were at summer camp, I attended a two-week class to study Yeats's poetry. Tim was twelve at the time, and when I returned, I regaled him and his sister with passionate stories of Ireland—its history, its literature—and my desire to study more poetry. I think that is what planted the Ireland seed in Tim, inspiring him to spend his junior year abroad at Trinity College in Dublin. Naturally, I was thrilled.

• • •

Bill drove me to Pilates today, worried I'm too fragile. He wanted me to join him for lunch with our friend Paul. After a brief hesitation, I agreed—I was fragile, raw, emotionally frayed. I go to sleep and wake up with thoughts of my lost boy. Why couldn't I help him? How do I make sense of a life cut short? I know I must somehow adjust to this loss, though it feels like a personal defeat. I do not want to let go. But why? Life continues, indifferent to the depth of my sorrow.

"This will pass," people say. No—it will never pass. I know they mean well, but nothing will make it better. I will never be okay again. And yet, somehow, I must find a way to move toward resilience—the ability, as Merriam-Webster defines it, to recover from or adjust to stress, change, or misfortune. Right now, I can't even imagine that.

Paul is patient, direct, and honest. "Let's have it," I say, picking at my turkey and provolone panini at Mediterraneo restaurant. He remembers the painful moments we've shared, the long, often difficult conversations about my son, and the ways those talks have slowly, quietly shaped my understanding and grief. Gently, he reminds me that none of it was my fault—that nothing I did, or could have done, would have changed the outcome. "The best predictor of future performance is past behavior," Paul says. "You will almost always be in a lose/lose situation with your son. If you try to care for him, he will be resentful, thinking you haven't done enough. If you do not react, he will be confused, maybe slow down a little—but still remain angry, because his mind believes no one ever does enough. Any kindness, any help, may provoke a negative response—sometimes delayed, sometimes immediate. He is the classic example of the dog that bites the hand that feeds it. Nothing you do will induce lasting change, though it may offer temporary relief."

Paul explains that Tim lived in psychotic depression, a biological illness. In the depths of his depression, his thinking was disordered, delusional. Emerging from it, he often lashed out, then apologized. He offered intermittent glimpses of positive behavior, which kept me tuned in. When depressed, he believed terrible things, despite clear evidence to the contrary. Mental illness operates in an alternate reality. He viewed his father--and in some ways himself--as defective.

Knowing this, I understand I must restart my living clock. It has been four weeks since he's gone. I must move forward—for me, for Bill, for our relationship, and for my health. Today is the 22nd, and I will give it my best shot. I will not reschedule the Mass. I cannot climb the stairs to St. Martha's Church because of my limited mobility. My daughter has a conflict and can't be here. I cannot wait and reschedule in a month or two when it fits her schedule, only to break down and relive the loss—it would be like ripping the bandage off a healing wound. Just listening to the lyrics is shattering:

"Danny Boy"

Oh Danny boy, the pipes, the pipes are calling
From glen to glen, and down the mountain side
The summer's gone, and all the flowers are dying
'Tis you, 'tis you must go and I must bide.
But come ye back when summer's in the meadow
Or when the valley's hushed and white with snow
'Tis I'll be here in sunshine or in shadow
Oh Danny boy, oh Danny boy, I love you so.
And if you come, when all the flowers are dying
And I am dead, as dead I well may be
You'll come and find the place where I am lying
And kneel and say an "Ave" there for me.
And I shall hear, tho' soft you tread above me
And all my dreams will warm and sweeter be
If you'll not fail to tell me that you love me
I'll simply sleep in peace until you come to me.
I'll simply sleep in peace until you come to me.

It's not just the notion of loss, but of someday being reunited, that's one of the reasons "Danny Boy" has never gone away. I did love him so. Final word: Even as I struggle, even as despair presses close, I remind myself: resilience is not the absence of grief. It is the small, deliberate act of standing, moving forward, breathing, despite the weight of the loss. Today, that is enough.

ELEVEN

RECOVERY

Day 35
He died five weeks ago, but I wasn't notified until the next day. I wonder if he knew I was in Boston—I had posted a single photo on social media, taken at an outdoor seaport restaurant. My life has changed forever. When do I stop counting? At first, it was days. Then weeks. Now, one month and one week. Or should I count from when he began to drift from us, eleven years ago?

It was also a shock—his perceptions, I had no idea, had been so far from reality. I tried to talk to him. I cried. I wondered how this could have happened. I was not willing to accept that mental illness was bigger than me, that I could not fix it. At the time, it was sad, but I held out hope. Now, it is even sadder, because hope is gone. Hope died when Tim left this planet.

I am grasping for anything—reading spiritual books, searching for meaning. I do not want to belong to a bereavement group. I cannot bear to hear or feel the pain of strangers. A son is a son until he gets himself a wife. I understand what that means, but it does not ease the loss.

I keep asking myself if I'm focusing on the wrong things. It has been more than five weeks, and still my daughter has not come. This is her family of origin, her brother, yet she stands apart from our grief, and her absence presses hard against my heart.

What I wanted was simple—to hold her hand, to hug her, to feel her beside me. Instead, she said, "I'll get back to you with possible dates." Perhaps she needs to grieve in her own way, alone—just when I needed her most.

• • •

I grieved not only for Tim, but for the family we had once been. I missed the deep connectedness that comes from being part of a family. But Tim wanted everyone to know he had suffered at the hands of his abusive father. He lived bound in bitterness and resentment, clinging to wounds inflicted by others. He spoke of his wife's verbal attacks and lack of understanding of an already fragile and gentle soul, unsure of himself. Part of him seemed strangely at ease in the role of victim.

Over time, he became narcissistic. He appeared indifferent to how his behavior affected others—his mother, his sister, perhaps even his wife. He did not seem willing to make the transition from victimhood to survivor. His mental illness escalated, and there was nothing I could do. You cannot change another person. You can offer help and advice, but the decision must be theirs. He was a married adult.

I offered to fund marital counseling, but he refused. Even after the divorce, when he tried to make amends and apologized for his behavior, the damage was already done. When his ex-wife moved the children out of Massachusetts, he allowed it, though I warned him it was a mistake. She promised he could visit anytime and even sleep on the couch, but her promises turned to lies—and then to threats. He gave in, and visitation and child support became an endless struggle.

Why do mothers—particularly me, a single parent for seventeen years—think we can intercede and fix everything? We can't. And yet I carried this weight always, believing it was my responsibility. What I have learned, painfully, is that love does not equal control, and even the deepest devotion cannot repair another's mind or choices. Strength lies not in fixing, but in knowing your limits, and finding a way to carry on even when the grief is unrelenting.

Psychology Today defines my situation:

A single parent is someone who is unmarried, widowed, or divorced and not remarried. The single-parent household can be headed by a mother, a father, a grandparent, an uncle, or aunt. According to the Pew Research Center, between 25 to 30 percent of children under age 18 in the U.S. live in a single-parent household. The U.S. Census reports that roughly 22 million children live with a single parent. And three times as many women, when compared with men, head these households.

Reading this description, it all sounds factual and do-able—but it leaves out a crucial truth: every decision about your child rests entirely on your shoulders. Balancing a full-time job while trying to attend every sports game or music recital feels nearly impossible, yet you do your best to give your children the life they deserve. *Psychology Today* doesn't mention that children want to feel safe and "just like everyone else"—to attend a baseball game with their father or go to the high-school father-daughter dance.

Daughters need fathers who love unconditionally, lis-ten actively, and support their dreams, showing affection and celebrating achievements. Sons look to their fathers for guidance and direction. When mental illness and er-ratic behavior enter the picture, as it did with my children's father, the challenges multiply. Financial hardship and the need to protect my children from the very person who should have loved and cared for them became an added burden as a single parent.

And how does a boy learn to be a man if not from his father? How does he learn structure, purpose, the basics—shaving, changing a tire, understanding sports—or simply gain encouragement to explore what gives life meaning? Despite my efforts, like playing catch after school, or taking Tim to sports events, I could not fully provide these experiences. In an attempt to restore Tim's "lost status," with financial help from his paternal grandmother and aunt, I enrolled him at The Dexter School for boys in Brookline, Mass., hoping the teachers could serve as father figures and provide guidance. The school was academically rigorous, offering courses like Latin and public speaking, with mandatory participation in all sports. I had hoped it would be transformative for Tim. In many ways it was—though in later years he admitted he despised it. (In 2013, Dexter School merged with its sister school, Southfield, to form Dexter Southfield.)

Raising children alone means assuming full accountability for every decision and every outcome. There is no partner to share the joys or sorrows, no other adult in the home to help shoulder the weight. It is an enormous task to try to get it right. I know I made mistakes as a single parent—perhaps I was too bossy or controlling, and I surely relied too heavily on my children for emotional support. Boundaries sometimes blurred because of my own needs. It is easy to become enmeshed when you are the only adult in the house. Mea culpa. Yet even as they grew into adulthood, I kept trying. I clung to hope: if I just did this, or if only I did that, perhaps he would find someone to love and then he would be okay. Hope strings a parent along.

Bill and I continued our regular visits to Boston, spending a week there every few months to be with family. By then, more than five years had passed since Tim's divorce was final.

> Mon, Dec 12, 2011 5:02 p.m.
> Hi Mom, Btw, next week I'm introducing u to my girlfriend. Love, Tim

> On Dec 12, 2011 6:57 p.m., "Susan Kelley" wrote:
> Can't wait. Any heads up on your girlfriend? Name, age?

> From: timothy To: Susan Kelley
> Sent: Mon, Dec 12, 2011 7:09 p.m.
> (she's from Cambodia). I'm at work, but will write more when I get home. I think she's the one. We only met recently, but I've a strong feeling. Think you'll know why when you meet her

> On Dec 13, 2011 8:20 a.m. "Susan Kelley" wrote:
> I am so happy for you Tim. Really looking

forward to seeing you and meeting your friend.
Love, Mom

Tue, Dec 13, 2011 at 10:43 a.m.
Thank u, mom. I am happy. You'll see what I
mean next week. :)

I was thrilled to hear he had a girlfriend who may even be "The ONE." Very excited to meet her. I started imagining a smart, educated young woman on the same intellectual level who appreciates Tim and will treat him with kindness. At Bill's suggestion I made a reservation to meet within walking distance to our hotel—Legal's Seafood on the waterfront.

Then came the day I met her. I don't think I had ever been so stunned at meeting anyone, especially given how particular my son usually was—always drawn to smart, pretty girls.

The person he introduced that evening had a deep voice and a medical port visible on their chest. A simple cardigan would have concealed the blatantly obvious focal point. They told us they had met on Match.com. The two of them held hands easily, as though already close. She ordered wine, he had a beer. She finished her own meal and then his.

Tim described her as an artist. Curious, I asked what medium she worked in. "Everything," she replied, "but I also do nails." She was Cambodian, had a child, and mentioned she had never been to the city before. It all felt so unlike Tim—the prep school graduate, the boy with lofty tastes. I couldn't help but wonder if he had checked all the wrong boxes on that dating site.

She explained that she was on a kidney transplant list, which accounted for the port I had noticed. In time, though, that connection faded, like so many others in Tim's search for companionship.

• • •

In the months that followed, I tried to help however I could, to listen, to be present. But Tim's situation was unraveling. At the time he was working for a financial institution in Boston, living alone in a shabby apartment in Quincy. I dreamed of moving him into a better place, fixing it up, creating some sense of stability for him.

Instead, he grew more erratic. Then he quit his job. At last, I gathered my courage and told him what I believed he needed to hear: "You need to get the correct diagnosis and start the proper medication."

My words set him off. He exploded: "Never contact me again. Stop treating me like I'm a mental patient."

And so began the long silence. Years passed while I held on to hope that he might change his mind. I only ever wanted to help, but it was not to be. I missed him then, and

I miss him still. I thought of him every single day.

And then:

Sent: Fri, Sep 20, 2013 3:05 p.m.

Subject: Goodbye

I had a meltdown at work on Wednesday and tendered my resignation, which was then accepted this afternoon, which I cannot believe given my state. This is a life ending scenario. Too much pain. I killed myself at this job, which was all I had. I don't have enough money for rent next month.

I am writing to say goodbye. I cannot take it anymore. Honestly, I can't believe this has happened. I cracked under the stress, true, after working way too hard.

The thing that troubles me the most is that I've always lived with the specter of my father's guilt. He did whatever the hell he wanted to do. No matter what. I might be a congenital fuck-up, but I have not taken the easy road. No one in the world understands let alone appreciates how hard it has been to try to put a good face on it, just to get through the day, when I've been dying inside all along. Tim

TWELVE

RELEASE

Day 39
Labor Day weekend. August 31. My mind still runs 24/7 with the *whys*—and with the love I carried for him. He had wanted to get married. I find myself telling Bill, yet again, the story: how I sold some of my jewelry to an auction and coin dealer, who eventually tracked down the oval diamond Tim's fiancée had requested. How I then brought the stone to a jeweler to have it crafted into the exact ring she had sketched.

And then I burst out, voice rising: "What mother does this? Me! I did everything possible for my kids, trying to make up for the lack of a normal dad. I know—it sounds like 'the list' again."

Bill rises from his chair, walks over, and steadies me with both hands on my shoulders. His eyes meet mine, calm but firm: "I cannot listen to these stories anymore. It's what made you sick in the first place. It's giving me high blood pressure because I worry about you. The constant rehash is awful, and I don't want to hear it again. It's toxic. Move forward—it's over. If you need to find someone professional to talk to, do that. But I won't listen to these stories anymore. They change nothing. We had good times with Tim. Remember Ireland, when he was such a wonderful tour guide? Either you accept the mental illness diagnosis, or you believe he was the most ungrateful son who ever lived. It's your choice. If you don't move forward, you're going to die. We don't have that much time left—we're eighty. How do you want to spend your remaining years?"

His words land like stones. I want to scream—loud enough to shake the world—because what I gave as a mother was never enough. No matter how hard I tried, it could never undo what Tim had inherited: the mental illness from his father, compounded by years of emotional torment. What *is* mental illness? We cannot see it, which makes it harder to recognize and harder still to treat.

Mental illness is a chronic disease. It is the number one untreated illness in the United States. And it carries a stigma. Left untreated, it nearly always worsens, and too often ends in suicide. If a diabetic doesn't take insulin, they can die. If someone has cancer, we respond with compassion: "I'm so sorry—I hope the treatment works." If someone breaks a bone, the injury is obvious, visible. No one blames a person for having diabetes or cancer. But mental illness?

It hides in plain sight. It's denied, minimized, judged. And that judgment can be fatal.

• • •

I call our friend Paul. I need help. Coming to my rescue once again, he brings me lunch from Walt's: fish and chips. He sits with me as I talk and cry. He listens to my stories: me saying Tim was okay before he married. I strive to live in the present moment, but in telling him, I see I am remembering other times and problems apparent since early years. Why else would I have taken him to a psychiatrist at age three? I am doing the blame game, and anger has fogged my logic.

Mental illness progresses in the twenties. This is what I saw with my ex-husband as well as my son. The delusions, the crazy thinking, fast talking, incorrect medication. My former mother-in-law had told me her son had been diagnosed with bipolar disorder as a teenager and he refused to take the prescribed medication. His behavior was very manic, and then he would sleep for days.

"Let go of the anger at the ex-wife," Paul says. "You are really angry and furious with your son, who treated you like crap for the past twenty-five years. You are projecting your anger onto the wrong people. Deal directly with your anger at Tim. He had a genetic and inherited mental illness. He was a tortured soul."

Day 49
Who am I angry at? Today, I cry. Paul tells me it's good—
that the tears are part of grieving, a way to desensitize
when every nerve ending feels raw and exposed.

Still, my energy is drained from circling the same
questions: Why don't Tim's now-adult children understand that all I ever did was try to help him? But if I'm
honest, I know that's not where my anger truly belongs.
Paul is right.

I am angry at *him*—at Tim—for putting me through
hell. My son, the one I loved so fiercely, turned against me
in the grip of his illness. And he did it because he could—
because he knew I would always be there, no matter what.
That love became my undoing. He told his wife and children that I had ruined his life, and they believed him.

This is where the tangle lies: Was it Tim, or was it the
illness? Do I blame the disease that hijacked his mind, or
do I blame the son who knew how deeply his words could
cut me? Guilt whispers that I should have done more,
tried harder, found a way to reach him. Blame shouts
that he turned on me, that he chose to hurt the one person who never abandoned him. I break down under the
weight of both.

● ● ●

Bill and I have an overflowing storage unit we've been meaning to clean out for years. Most of the boxes have been sitting there for nearly two decades, their contents half-forgotten, except for the ones I know hold copies of my published books and bins of family photographs.

We hire an organizer with a truck to help us. One by one, cardboard boxes and plastic bins are hauled out and set before us. The first box I open, a photograph slips into my lap—Tim at about seven years old, wearing his gray suit, white shirt, and tie for his First Communion. I smile at the memory. He and his sister made their First Communion together, and it was such a joyous day. At the time they were attending St. Peter's Catholic School in Cambridge, but the nuns were too rigid, too unyielding. They wanted out, so I soon transferred them to Peabody Grammar School—a much better fit.

In another envelope marked "*Italy,*" I find photos from when Tim visited us after 9/11, leaving his wife and child behind. So many snapshots of Florence, of museums we explored together, of evenings meeting up with Bill in his studio. Those were happy days, carefree and warm. The tears come immediately.

Then I see a bin marked in large block letters: *TIM.* Inside are photographs from the wedding shower I hosted for his fiancée in Boston, with all the relatives gathered. The wedding invitation, too, and pictures from a celebration I once remembered as filled with hope. A marriage that un-raveled almost as soon as it began.

Bill pulls me close and says gently, "Another time you can go through these, maybe even let some of them go—but it's too soon now."

And he is right.

But still, the question looms: What do I do with all of it—his photos, his diplomas, the keepsakes I had saved for the day he found a new apartment, a day that will never come?

I don't know what the next chapter is supposed to be. Rage, sadness, repetition, and outbursts circle through me like a storm. First came the shock—the suddenness of los-ing someone who had been part of my life for fifty-five years. My child. My son. The baby who came from my body, who drank milk from my breasts, his tiny head rest-ing against my chest. I can still remember that baby scent, that overwhelming closeness.

I never knew I could love another human being so com-pletely. And now I am left on a journey I never wanted to take.

The infamous five stages of grief were introduced by Elisabeth Kübler-Ross, a Swiss-American psychiatrist, in her 1969 book, *On Death and Dying*. The model was initially developed to describe the emotional experience of terminally ill patients coming to terms with their mortality, not for those grieving the loss of a loved one, yet I apply them here as I feel they are appropriate:

Denial: When I received the email from the police detective to call about my son, I did not want to hear it.

Anger: I am furious that his disease turned him into a different person. But it's ridiculous to be angry at a person for dying and also to be angry at yourself for not being able to fix it.

Bargaining: Does not apply in this case. But it used to, when I would think, "If I just do this…"

Depression: Unending.

Acceptance: Not gonna happen.

• • •

There is no such thing as justice for all. I remind myself of this, even as I struggle to release my own need for justice on a personal level. It should not be my burden to carry. I was a good mother. I loved my son and did everything I could to help him heal. He sent me emails filled with both gratitude and complaint—thanking me on some days, blaming his marriage on others. But what did he say about me to her? His wife and children only ever knew one side of the story, told straight from him in the depths of depression, when he believed those distorted thoughts to be true.

And so I grieve not only for the loss of my son, but also for the estrangement that came before it. I rage at being cut off from my grandchildren, at being shut out of their lives. The injustice of it burns. Can it be rectified? Probably not.

But I know I cannot live in that rage. I will try, with my whole heart, to release it to karma. I will try to practice kindness and forgiveness, even when my pain tempts me otherwise. I will not send his ex-wife the final text my son wrote to me. That is not who I am, and nothing I send will bring him back.

• • •

There are so many grief triggers, and I am desperate for relief—searching endlessly, almost obsessively, on Google. That's when I come across something called *cord cutting*.

Cord cutting is a way to spiritually sever your connections to people or situations that sap your energy, and you don't have to have magical training to do it—all you need are your thoughts. The purpose is to release the emotional cargo and move forward. I need to let go of the attachment, the guilt, the sorrow, emotional rawness. The act is thought to release negative energies or attachments that may be hindering personal growth or causing emotional pain. This can be a symbolic or ritualistic act aimed at creating emotional distance or freedom. It is supposed to give me back all the energy that I have spent worrying about Tim for fifty-five years.

Have I lost my mind?

Probably; but I hope only temporarily. I am going to explore this cord cutting so I may get on with my life. I cannot bring my son back, but I do need my energy back. So much energy. I will try cutting the cord with great love and sadness for Tim. I need to move forward and let him go.

According to the website:

- Physically, cord cutting may lead to a reduced sense of stress and tension in interactions with the individual for both you and the other person.
- Mentally, it can contribute to a more balanced and detached perspective, promoting a healthier dynamic for the both of you. The website says:
  "It's essential to approach cord cutting with mindfulness of its potential effects, fostering a space for positive transformations for both of you."

I order a roll of rope cord and white and black candles on Amazon, as directed, but I am unable to do it—to cut off my son. It would be like getting an annulment. I shove it all in a kitchen drawer, and of course I don't tell Bill.

• • •

Bouncing back. I always thought of myself as the resilient warrior. For years, my children were my inspiration and my driving force. But now, that part of me feels lost. I believe I have reached what many would call rock bottom—the "nothing left to lose" stage. From here, the only way is up.

I have cried until I was emptied out. I have felt the pain, and I am facing reality. Tears are the release I have. I tell myself he is at peace, and that has to be enough. I know I must step away from the darkness that surrounds me. The cloud is too heavy, too raw. When I try to talk about it, the words burn in my throat. I attempt to rationalize that death is a transition, not a tragedy—but believing it is another struggle altogether.

And yet—I am alive. I can breathe. I am in a clinical trial that reminds me to focus on the positive. Joy. Love. Gratitude. Peace. These must become my anchors. I remind myself to stand back up, because I have reasons: a devoted and loving husband who has held me up through all of this, a daughter who is my heart, stepdaughters and grandchildren who bring light to my days.

What's gone is gone. To keep staring backward is to lose the present. All I truly have is *now*. Forgive. Let it go. I think of Tim's ex-wife, of how much anger I hold toward her, of how I want to blame her. But blame only makes me a victim. If I keep driving by looking in the rearview mirror, I will crash. The past cannot be rewritten, and no amount of revisiting it will bring him back.

THIRTEEN

REBOOT

Day 52

As Viktor Frankl, Austrian neurologist, psychologist, and Holocaust survivor, said, "When we are no longer able to change a situation, we are challenged to change ourselves." My new mantra.

It's a passage of the soul—because we can't give up and we have to move forward. After mourning comes rebalance, rebuilding, and rebooting.

You must rewire your brain to a new way of thinking. For me, that has meant a lot of soul-searching and reading—to avoid feeling like I've failed as a mom. Today, I feel pushed and pulled into a new chapter. F. Scott Fitzgerald said, "Life starts all over again when it gets crisp in the fall." It's not exactly crisp fall weather here in Florida, but to me, fall has always symbolized new beginnings and starting over.

And today is Friday the 13th—a date that holds deep significance for me. On a Friday the 13th in October 1972, I walked out of that marriage with my two cherished babies, a box of Pampers, and my grandmother's jewelry, left to me as a keepsake. I have always thought of that as my second luckiest day—Friday the 13th.

Every day is a new day. A new story. It's time to release the old story that brings pain. I need to grieve this loss alone—and then let it go. No one can erase my many happy memories of Tim: the laughter, the fun, the joy of being together. I will treasure these always.

By chance, I stumbled upon Dr. Joe Dispenza online. A neuroscience researcher, international lecturer, corporate consultant, meditation teacher, and New York Times bestselling author, he has helped thousands rewire the way they think, feel, and heal. One of his most quoted lines struck me immediately: "Your thoughts can make you sick. But your thoughts can also make you well."

His message is simple yet profound—the mind holds the power to heal the body. His words spoke to something deep inside me, a possibility I hadn't dared to imagine before. He writes about "rebooting" and "rewiring" the brain, about reshaping thought itself. I realized this was exactly what I needed: a fresh path, a new lens through which to see my life and my grief.

Dispenza offers more than ideas—he offers hope, practical tools, and the reminder that transformation, even after unimaginable loss, is possible. And in this moment, I find myself reaching for that guidance.

I like what he says: "Create a new personal reality. Become so conscious of what you think. Make a decision. Do not go back to the emotional past. Familiarize yourself with a new way of thinking. The new voice in your head."

He explains that most people spend 70 percent of their lives in survival mode—constantly anticipating the worst-case scenario based on the past. "Do you want to live in the past or in the present?" he asks. "If you keep thinking about the past, your energy goes there. You can be angry, but return to the present moment. Surrender the past in order to go forward. Recondition your body every day—without fear."

He teaches that when we recall a painful event, our body produces the same chemistry we experienced at the time. Let it go, he urges. "Your thoughts create your destiny. The same thoughts lead to the same choices, which lead to the same emotions. Make the choice to change."

This makes sense to me. Every time I recall the events of Tim, I produce the same chemistry—stress hormones flooding my system. I need to consciously decide to make different choices. According to Dispenza, it takes forty-five days to create new neural pathways.

I am searching for ways to heal my altered state. Friends are telling me I must keep my attention on the larger picture, my health—the clinical trial—and remind myself that compared with the recovery of my health, everything else is insignificant. Healing is my responsibility. I cannot bring my son back. I must learn to live with the loss and not use all my energy being sad and going backward. Stay in the present and plan for the future. It's a mental adjustment. With time, I will stop asking "why" and begin asking "how"—how to live with the weight of memory,

The worst thing that could possibly happen has happened to me. All I can hope for now is to reach a place where I can live with it. I do not see myself as a victim. I have no room for anger, no energy to spend judging whether this loss is unjust. My task is forgiveness—saving what strength I have for the present, rather than endlessly replaying the past.

There is no quick fix for grief. It is a process you move through, intense and isolating—the loneliest walk you will ever take. The mood swings, the tears, the sleepless nights, the constant circling of "what ifs" all weigh on me. I struggle to accept that my son is gone, and though I did everything in my power, I could not save him. Eventually, I had to let him go.

In the silence that follows loss, I knew I needed help. I searched for grief support and discovered the Alliance of Hope, an organization for suicide loss survivors. Their mission is to provide healing support to those coping with the shock, excruciating grief, and complex emotions of this kind of loss. They offer comfort, guidance, and resources, as well as a 24/7 online forum overseen by mental health counselors and trained volunteers.

I reached out because I needed to talk with someone who could truly understand, and I made an appointment with Ronnie, a therapist who is herself a survivor. She listened for an hour and a half, kind and compassionate, allowing me to tell my story without judgment. At the end, she reassured me with words I didn't know I needed to hear: My son died of terminal mental illness. It was not a failure of my parenting. It was an illness that overwhelmed him.

Her words did not erase the grief or lighten the loss, but they gave me something vital to hold on to—the permission to forgive myself.

Ronnie suggested I join a support group for parents who have lost a child to suicide. It is another gift the Alliance of Hope offers, but for now, I hesitate. I do not want a companion in grief. Perhaps someday. Instead, I hold on to one of their simplest tools: gratitude. I choose to be grateful that my son was in my life, for the years we had as a family, for the joy of our trips to Ireland while he was in school, for every moment before the illness consumed him. Those memories are mine to keep, and no one can take them away.

I will always be thankful that he was born, thankful that I got to love him for as long as I did. I will always grieve the pain he endured, but I will also cherish the real Tim—the son I knew before the shadows grew too heavy.

• • •

Suicide adds shock, trauma, loneliness, and many complicated emotions. I may never know the results of the toxicology report, but I will always know the truth: my son took his own life. Not to hurt anyone else, but because he could no longer go on. In those final moments, he wasn't thinking about anyone but the unbearable weight of his despair. He had fallen into such darkness that rational "choice" was no longer possible. Suicide is, in many ways, the most tragic form of death—leaving behind shock, questions without answers, and a heavy stigma that settles on those who remain.

When I am not crying on the outside, I am crying on the inside. My body feels consumed by pain and sadness, ready to ignite at the slightest trigger. I always thought of myself as strong, even lucky. But now it feels as if a black cloud hovers over me.

Bill tells me I am strong, that I am capable of healing and forgiveness. Yet it is hard to let go of the need for someone to take responsibility, for some acknowledgment of guilt or wrongdoing. It is not my place to prove to my ex-daughter-in-law that she was wrong to keep me from my grandchildren, but I struggle with the temptation—always one email away from laying blame at her feet. And yet, I don't know her side. Bill reminds me often: "There are two sides to every story, and then there's the truth." Sometimes I think my son was skilled at playing us against each other—blaming her to me, blaming me to her—while never fully owning his part.

In my grief, I have forgotten those words of wisdom about the "two sides and the truth in the middle."

Women often marveled that I had the courage to walk away in 1972 with no money and two small children. They told me that it's the risks you take—and the courage to take them—that become the making of your life. But to me, it wasn't about courage; it was life or death.

In those early years, I thought sometimes of remarriage, but the right person did not appear. Instead, I worked, went back to school, and poured myself into raising my children. They were smart, funny, and wonderful, and I preferred their company to that of most men I dated. Many men struggled to handle my son's challenges, and those men did not last. The three of us were the deal. We built a life together.

That determination carried me far. At fifty-six, I returned to college, completing and earning my degree from Simmons in Boston. I even hired a math tutor when I needed one, but I didn't give up. I was determined, and I persisted. Long before that, I had pursued my dream of becoming a published author, even when my own mother told me, "You're not the writer in the family." Not only did I write one book, I wrote many—and I ended up on the *Today* show and on *Oprah* as an author and expert.

I wanted the best for my children and did everything in my power to make sure they had the education and the opportunities they deserved. I refused to let my mistakes dictate their future. I left their father when I knew I had to, and I worked tirelessly to create a better life. I never gave up on them. I never gave up on my son. I held onto hope that he would one day see the light and heal, that he would find his way through.

But that miracle never came. And so, despite every success, every risk I took, every dream I chased down with sheer will, I am left standing in this truth: I am a mother who could not save her son. Nothing else matters beside that fact.

And so life goes on. But it is different because my son is gone, and I will never see him again. No, I do not think any good will come of this, but as Bill said, "It's over." Tim tried twice before to end his life and spoke of doing so numerous other times. Who am I to insist that he owed it to his children or to me and his sister to persist in his unhappiness?

As Tim's mental health deteriorated, his emails became more tormented, accusatory, self-pitying, self-hating, and isolated.

Sun, Jun 10, 2012 at 7:40 p.m.

Dear mom,

I do sincerely appreciate your considered reply. I do wish to make one final point (and will spare you anything further on the topic), which is that it's not the past that piques me, but, rather, the present. I believe I may have expressed to you that the most difficult thing to express in Larry's abuse was the impersonal nature with which it was dispensed -- I was the child in the photograph in his movie before I was his child. In brief, I never had more than a walk-on role in the psychodrama that was his life, and it is the absurd meaninglessness of that suffering that is most difficult to brook, the indelible mark. . . .

To return to the present, I found myself in a very difficult situation at work not too long ago that caused me again to fear the loss of my job. Again, it was the impersonal nature of the experience, and the treatment meted me that was most difficult to take. I mean, I live a marginal existence with few comforts and little relief. Forget how I got here, what I have done, or may not have done to get here ... on a good day, it's nearly too much to take. But I came to the realization, correct or not, that I don't deserve it. Perhaps it would be more correct to say that I don't want it. Falls short of a religious epiphany, I know, but I decided I'm done sacrificing, done accommodating, done apologizing, done asking ... and, most of all, done listening, if listening doesn't result in my (reciprocally) being heard. I'm done doing all but the bare minimum at this stage. No more dog and pony acts....

When asked to explain the meaning of the title of his book *Naked Lunch*, William S. Burroughs explained that it refers to "a frozen moment when everyone sees what is on the end of every fork." Not a religious epiphany at all, but a vision of reality -- a vision of the present -- that is all too clear and, as it were, all too bleak. What I'm referring to here has little to do with my job or living situation, and, rather, everything to do with relationships. I was an obedient (if not obeisant) child and for the better part of my life the faithful good soldier. And I don't think anyone has ever recognized that, let alone truly appreciated that. More pressingly, I feel terribly alone and, worse, that I have always been alone. The largess to which you refer [was] always coupled with words or gestures gauged to impress upon me that they were anything but charity. And I deserve -- and did deserve -- to be treated with greater dignity than that.

I can no longer brook the illusion -- brook the lie. It has all but crushed me. I remember being called in to pay my final respects to your father as he lay dying. Final respects to a man who never made the slightest effort to get to know me, indeed, who could barely hide the contempt he felt for me, which, of course, was contempt projected onto me as a mere proxy in place of my father. To his credit (I suppose), he was able to fill the empty space between us briefly, albeit with a "world needs ditch diggers too" monologue (eerily reminiscent of Ted Knight's famous line in Caddy Shack). Absurd to the point of being almost unworldly in contrast to the general atmosphere of pathos that day, his attitude toward me really drove home my own inconsequence even in relation to my own "family."

I really don't ever want to hear about your mother ever again. Her life is over. And it wasn't such a bad life. And yet she still has any number of people jumping through hoops for her. Of course, she is merely exemplary of what I'm referring to, which is that I've always lived at the margins of my so-called life, lived as a walk on in any number of dramas. But I finally do get it -- I don't count. Was I a squeaky wheel at age

6 when I was being abused, or were the adults in my life completely self-absorbed and out to lunch, put out by a child/grandchild that they conceived? Was I unreasonable to think that my sibling should hold me in higher regard than her friends and not think of me as a liability? Maybe? Who knows ... What I do know is that losing me is of far greater consequence to you and to M., than my losing either of you. I'm just a middle-aged loser with a shitty job living in a basement. You're the relationship expert, and she's, well, saving the world (saving the rest of the world). But, somehow, neither expert could preserve one of the closest relationships in her life. I've done my soul searching already, and you would do best to do some of your own.
Love, Tim

Thu, Aug 9, 2012 at 1:37 p.m.

Tim
Here is the name of a very good psychiatrist who has been highly recommended by my doctor of 42 years, in Boston. Why not see if you can get an appointment with him. I think he could be very helpful and could also discuss what would be the right medication for you. Please, it's worth a shot and I hope you try this. I would so love to see my son a happy man.
Love, Mom
[Referral to a distinguished psychiatrist]

Sent: Sun, May 26, 2013 11:07 a.m.

Mom
Stop treating me like the perpetual mental patient. You do me no service, and you do yourself no service. You've treated me as a liability since I was a child up through to the present time. If you were honest with yourself, you would see how treating me as such, really, serves you. It grates on me to no end, this chronic disrespect. Do you forget that I was there for you through Kevin's illness? My uncle, yes, but a man whom I saw maybe four times in my life? (Who am I to mourn your father, your brother, where you made no real attempt

to assimilate me into what was and is entirely your family?) Or the hours that I spent talking to you about writing a book of essays, something beyond the relationship books? No, of course not.

You have no respect for me, and never had. In truth, dismissing me as a mental patient (or some kind of smart ass when I try to speak openly and honestly to you) is your way of dealing --or, rather-- of not dealing with a myriad of your own issues. To keep to the present, you don't respect me because I don't fulfill some image you have of a successful, respectable person. I've tried to show my love and good faith in doing, but also in adopting your speech in the hope that I might understand and might myself be understood. But I see that in trying to do so I have done wrong by you as well as myself because I've not challenged your view which I believe is distorted and that I believe you know to be fundamentally distorted.

And it hurts, being so easily dismissed by one's own parent. What is even more difficult to accept is my own complicity (my own duplicity) in perpetuating this dynamic, which will now come to an end. To keep with the recent past, you never really invited me into your life, nor were you ever really willing to accept me and

> my life on equal terms, to accept my beliefs and
> values and experiences.
> Please stop contacting me. Tim

This ended our communication for eleven years. Yet even during that long silence, I thought of him always. Now, I know I must forgive myself and find a way to move forward. I am grateful to have been in Boston when he died. And despite the nightmare of standing next to the cardboard box that held his body, I know I will survive.

I no longer cry three times a day, or every time I look at a photo of him—though there are many scattered throughout my home. Sometimes, I speak to him aloud, saying the words I never could before: I am so sorry you suffered. I have tried to stop the endless ruminating, the rehashing, the recriminations. Reliving moments that are over only fuels anxiety; it does nothing to heal. I am learning to let go of what I cannot change and to hold close the memories that bring light rather than pain.

Day 65
September 26, 2024. I am a realist. I do not drift into "magical thinking" that my son will return. Emotionally, I am doing better, yet I think of him every day. Sometimes a memory even makes me grin.

When Tim was at Choate in Connecticut and prom season rolled around, I asked him on a phone call if he had a date. He said no, but he was planning something "special" with a friend. He even asked me to order the *Saturday Night Fever* album—the one with John Travolta in his iconic white suit, black shirt, and pointed collar.

As it turned out, his plan was brilliant. He and his tech-savvy friend wired the auditorium with speakers, and at the height of the evening, the lights suddenly went out. Shiny disco balls dropped from the ceiling, *"Stayin' Alive"* blasted through the room, and out strutted Tim—dressed head to toe as Travolta. He had rented the costume, rehearsed the moves, and delivered his performance perfectly. The faculty thought it was hilarious, so he didn't even get into trouble. I only wish I could have been there.

Today, though, was different. At home in Florida, with Hurricane Helene on the horizon, Bill was playing old Clancy Brothers Irish rebel songs. I was in the kitchen making chicken salad for lunch, silently hoping we wouldn't lose power in the storm. Then the music washed over me, and a wave of sadness followed. I thought of Tim in Ireland—how happy he had seemed there, almost as if he had found a home, at least for a little while. The memories opened the floodgates. I broke into uncontrollable sobs, tears blurring my vision and splashing into the bowl. I suppose that will happen sometimes.

Tim studied in Ireland for three years. Ever the academic, he even learned Irish Gaelic—no easy task, as it is far from a romance language. I can still see him pulling little cards from his pockets, covered with translations and verb conjugations. His dedication paid off: he earned an MPhil in Irish Studies, majoring in Anglo-Irish literature and minoring in Modern Irish language and literature.

I miss him—his wry wit, his sharp mind, the way he always understood me without explanation. I will hold on to those good times forever. Perhaps I could not fully heal while he was alive. But now, I will. I am choosing to focus on positivity—the mind-body connection. I am stronger than the disease. I have love in my life, and I still have hope. If negativity once weighed me down and worsened my illness, then positivity can help me rise.

My defeatist attitude has no place here anymore. It is time to reclaim my power, to rebuild my strength, and to welcome healing. I believe in miracles—even though there was no miracle for Tim. I love this quote from another of Tim's favorite children's books:

> *You become. It takes a long time. That's why it doesn't happen often to people who break easily, or have sharp edges, or who have to be carefully kept. Generally, by the time you are Real, most of your hair has been loved off, and your eyes drop out and you get loose in your joints and very shabby. But these things don't matter at*

*all, because once you are Real you can't be ugly,
except to people who don't understand.*

—Margery Williams,
The Velveteen Rabbit, 1922

Grief is hard, but what feels even harder is being among others and pretending to be okay. I know it isn't their fault, and I don't expect them to fix it. The truth is, there are no rules for grieving.

FOURTEEN

RESCUE

Day 72

Good friends are rare, and in times of deep sorrow, they feel like lifelines. We are blessed to have Paul, who has known us for years. Because he already knows my story, I don't have to spend precious energy retelling it. Instead, I can lean on his wisdom as he helps me through this labyrinth of grief.

As a loving father himself, Paul instinctively understands what it would mean to lose a child. He doesn't need me to explain the depth of that pain. When he offered to come and sit with me again, I thought I was looking for answers. I asked him what could have finally driven my son to give up for good. But Paul saw past my words. He heard the guilt woven through them. With quiet clarity, he said: *"It's only your fault if you continue to let it be your fault."*

His words settled over me like both a rebuke and a mercy—reminding me that I cannot change what happened, but I can decide whether to carry the blame forever.

I find this quote:

> *The loneliest moment in someone's life is when they are watching their whole world fall apart, and all they can do is stare blankly. It's not the shattering itself that breaks you—it's the silence that follows, the quiet space where you realize there's nothing left to salvage. And in that moment, you know that you'll never be the same again. You'll build something new, perhaps, but it will never be what you lost.*

> — F. Scott Fitzgerald,
> *Of Love and Loneliness*

Day 85
I think I am back on track. I feel optimistic about my health and convinced—at least most days—that I'm getting the drug, not the placebo, in this blind clinical trial. Still, I can't help but turn over, again and again, the known and unknown facts of my son's death.

I've just had my fourth of ten doses at the Mayo Clinic in Jacksonville. No bad reactions so far, and I've been feeling fine. It's a five-hour drive each way. On the way home to Sarasota, we stop at our usual halfway point for gas and a restroom break. I'm stiff from the car ride and eager to get to the ladies' room.

"Cane or walker?" I ask Bill. He chooses the walker for stability and pulls it from the trunk. We make our way up the handicap ramp. An attractive middle-aged woman holds the door open for us. Bill is right behind me. And then, without warning, my recently injected right leg collapses. My ankle twists, my knee buckles, and I'm going down.

Bill grabs me. The woman does too. I never hit the ground, but the pain is blinding—shooting through my right quadriceps and ankle. Unbearable. I'm convinced I've broken my femur.

"Can you walk if we get you up on the walker?" the woman asks. She tells me she's a nurse. But I can't move. They sit me on the walker's seat, Bill runs for ice, and together they get me back to the car. No, I never make it to the ladies' room.

We drive the remaining two and a half hours to Sarasota Memorial Emergency, where we spend five more hours. X-rays confirm a broken ankle and a quadriceps sprain. They send me home in a knee boot, in a wheelchair. A major setback.

Day 95

My daughter is finally here. Despite promising myself I would keep it together, I break down at the sight of her. This is our first visit since Tim's death. I am still recovering at home from my recent fall and am immobile, so this will not be the visit I had envisioned.

We sit and chat. She keeps herself composed, saying simply that it is very sad. We talk about the past—fun times, and moments when we knew he was troubled.

She recalls a strange incident from Tim's high school years. He was home from prep school for the weekend, and on Sunday—the day he was to return—he told me he couldn't go back because his knee was painful and he was limping. I was annoyed, asking why he hadn't mentioned it sooner, but of course, I could not let him go back. I called a friend of mine, a physician at Children's Hospital in Boston, asking whether I should take Tim to the ER or get a referral. He got us in to see a top orthopedist immediately.

The knee was x-rayed, and the doctor told me my son had a needle in his kneecap. The doctor removed it arthroscopically and handed it to me in a plastic cup. I asked Tim if he had knelt on a floor where he might have picked it up. He said he didn't know. He stayed home for a few days, and then I drove him back to school in Connecticut. That was the end of it—or so I thought.

When I first told Paul this story, he suggested, "Have you considered that he may have put it there himself?" I had been shocked.

"No," I responded. "Why would he hurt himself intentionally?"

In retelling the story to my daughter, before I finished, she said quietly, "Maybe he put it there himself." "But why would he?" I asked. Then she reminded me of a sex abuse scandal at his school that had come out in the newspapers years later. Perhaps he didn't want to go back. But why didn't he tell me?

After she leaves to go for a run, I immediately turn on my laptop and search for "sex abuse scandal at Choate Rosemary Hall." Sure enough: *The New York Times*, *Boston Globe*—it's all over the internet. Choate Rosemary Hall apologizes for sexual misconduct spanning four decades, from 1963 to 2010.

> From *The New York Times*:
> [. . .] The report names 12 former faculty members who it says abused students, both male and female. In some cases, faculty members had sexual relationships with students for months, some of which continued after the students left the school. [. . .] Of the 12 former faculty members identified, three are dead. The New York Times tried to contact

the remaining nine on Thursday evening, but none responded. [. . .] For years, the school kept allegations of sexual misconduct from getting out, according to the report. "Sexual misconduct matters were handled internally and quietly," it said. "Even when a teacher was terminated or resigned in the middle of the school year because he or she had engaged in sexual misconduct with a student, the rest of the faculty was told little and sometimes nothing about the teacher's departure and, when told, was cautioned to say nothing about the situation if asked."

I will never know, of course, if Tim experienced sexual abuse while at boarding school. He was a beautiful boy, already marked by bullying in his younger years, and he would have been an easy target. If there was abuse, it would have been another trauma layered on top of what he already carried—mental illness compounded by wounds no child should endure. His inherited brain disorder was not within his control, but trauma could only have worsened it.

These thoughts open yet another door of worry and sorrow. My mind travels back through time, questioning everything. I think of the babysitters who watched my children when I worked or when I tried to date. Were they safe? Did I leave them in good hands? How can any mother ever be sure? I begin making mental lists of the people, turning over each memory, wondering if I missed something, if there were signs I didn't see.

Day 106
November 6, 2024 The Confirmation of Cause arrives today, and I am alone at home, still recovering from my fall.

I knew in my heart what the result would be—a mother's intuition shaped by years of experience. Tim lived for his children. His first text response to me in eleven years, on his birthday in June, had already hinted at trouble. The detective in Boston told us that he had recently visited his children and that the visit "did not go well." I can only imagine how this must have triggered a downward spiral—from despair to self-destruction. He was exhausted, and the struggle had left him hopeless.

I had been unable to access information about how Tim died. His adult sons would communicate only minimally, just enough to allow Bill and me a brief visit at the funeral home. I had ordered a death certificate one week after his death, but it listed no cause. I needed closure, verification.

I waited the ninety days for the toxicology report. At the end of October, I ordered another death certificate, hoping for definitive answers.

Heart pounding, I delicately open the business-size envelope, remove the paper, and unfold it. I run my finger down the lines, slowly absorbing the words:

Cause of Death: Overdose, non-prescription medication.

ACUTE DIPHENHYDRAMINE INTOXICATION.

Diphenhydramine is an antihistamine found in some allergy and sleep medicines, like Tylenol PM. He had ingested the contents of a bottle of Tylenol PM twenty years ago in his second attempt.

Slowly and painstakingly, hands trembling, I read both sides of the death certificate before my eyes land on the next line:

"Other significant conditions contributing to death but not resulting in underlying cause."

And then, on the right side, in a box outlined in heavy black ink:

Manner of death: SUICIDE.

Even though I had expected it, the reality hits hard—permanence. He is gone. I will never see him again.

The time of death is listed as "99:99." I google it and learn it indicates that the time of death is completely unknown. I was in Boston. Could I have stopped it if I had insisted on contacting him? Or would I have felt responsible for pushing him further? *Stop torturing yourself. It's over.*

Had he left a note? His children must have been shattered. Will they blame themselves? I will never know. When Tim chose to leave this world, the pain must have been unbearable, the sense of hopelessness complete. I can only believe he saw no other way to find peace.

I have the facts. I understand, in broad strokes, what happened. And I know it unfolded over many years. I must go on, though any thought that I could enjoy life again without survivor's guilt feels impossible right now.

Among the Irish writers Tim loved, Samuel Beckett was at the very top of his list. One quote, in particular, resonates deeply with me, from Samuel Beckett as he writes in *The Unnamable*: "You must go on. I can't go on. I'll go on."

Beckett's words capture a philosophy that reflects life itself: that failure and struggle are essential parts of an artist's—and perhaps anyone's—journey. First appearing in his 1953 play *Waiting for Godot*, this sentiment has become a symbol of endurance amid seemingly hopeless circumstances.

Another quote that strikes me as equally poignant is from Joseph Campbell: *"We must let go of the life we have planned, so as to accept the one that is waiting for us."*

Together, these words remind me that life's challenges—its loss, pain, and unpredictability—can be met with persistence and openness. They speak to the necessity of continuing forward, even when the path is unclear, and of embracing the life that unfolds before us, however unexpected it may be.

FIFTEEN

Resolution

Death is irrevocable; there is no calling it back. It cannot be undone. One of the most difficult truths about suicide—rarely spoken of—is the shadow of disgrace it can cast. Mental illness carries a similar stigma, and together they deepen the wounds in our already broken hearts. An insensitive statement can leave us in fear that our child's memory will be forever shadowed by how they died. A careless or insensitive comment can make us fear that our child's memory will be reduced to how they died rather than how they lived.

I choose to move forward in my journey, even if Tim did not choose to come along. That means letting go, again and again. What I have learned is this: we can do everything we believe is right and still lose them. It is heartbreaking. Yet I must learn to live in a world without someone I loved so deeply. And I will. If I need to restart and refocus a thousand times, I will.

I no longer want to carry guilt. Instead, I try to see death as a passage, a changeover. I remind myself that Tim's pain is gone. I picture him free, happy, and at peace. I know now that I could not change him or his final act. The only change I can make is within myself. My choice is to focus on what is still good and life-giving. My choice is joy.

I have let myself feel the anger, the fear, the blame—all of it coursing through my body. I have processed those emotions, and now I release them. What remains is the work of rebounding—not bouncing back with false cheer, but rising slowly, learning to accept what is.

I am practicing forgiveness: forgiveness for Tim, who never asked to be born into a life shadowed by mental illness; forgiveness for myself, for the ways dysfunction shaped our family. I want to let go of the trauma and the painful memories, holding onto love instead.

Buddhism teaches that nothing destroys us more quickly than our own minds. We are urged to release what we cannot control and tend to what we can. I would urge anyone to try to live this way. I only wish I had learned to believe it sooner.

SIXTEEN

RENAISSANCE

Day 109
NOVEMBER 9, 2024

I am the curator of my story. From here forward, I will guide it where I want it to go. Each day, I will choose what matters and what defines me as my life evolves. This is my world to experience, and it will be different now—because I am different.

The grief and sorrow have, at times, been unbearable. Yet in the midst of that pain, I have found solace in remembering my son with love. I will cherish those moments of joy, his wit, his flashes of wisdom. In the rubble of loss, I have discovered resilience, love, and the strength to step forward.

Reading through Tim's emails reminds me that his illness had a biological root, one that advanced despite every effort to fight it—through diagnoses, through treatments, through his courage. It was always an uphill battle. And yet, in those words, I find myself beginning to forgive myself. I see more clearly now that I was his cheerleader, his steady presence, his biggest fan. Still, he suffered in ways I could not reach, and he felt alone. That recognition floods me with compassion for him.

A meditation I read says healing begins with small steps: a steady breath, a gentle stretch, a grounding moment. These practices create tiny spaces of calm where peace can enter. Every breath, every pause, is an act of care—a way of reminding the body and spirit that safety and possibility still exist.

I am not sure why I saved so many of his emails, but today, when I typed his name into my inbox, I found a folder labeled "TIM," sitting just beneath my annual "TAX" file. The messages span from 2009 to 2013, the year he stopped writing to me. As I read, it is as if he returns—his voice, his humor, his wisdom, his struggles. I smile at the joy in some of them. I ache at the loneliness in others. In time, his words grow darker, edging into the language of psychosis. Still, they are pieces of him, pieces of us, and they remind me of the depth of his fight.

Ernest Hemingway once said:

> "In our darkest moments, we don't need solutions or advice. What we yearn for is simply human connection—a quiet presence,

a gentle touch. These small gestures are the anchors that hold us steady when life feels like too much.

Please don't try to fix me. Don't take on my pain or push away my shadows. Just sit beside me as I work through my own inner storms. Be the steady hand I can reach for as I find my way.

My pain is mine to carry, my battles mine to face. But your presence reminds me I'm not alone in this vast, sometimes frightening world. It's a quiet reminder that I am worthy of love, even when I feel broken.

So, in those dark hours when I lose my way, will you just be here? Not as a rescuer, but as a companion. Hold my hand until the dawn arrives, helping me remember my strength.

Your silent support is the most precious gift you can give. It's a love that helps me remember who I am, even when I forget."

To my friends and relatives, I offer my gratitude. Your silent support is the most precious gift, a love in its purest form.

Day 148
December 18, 2024
There was an email this morning from a former coworker of my son: *"Peace, Merry Christmas. Regina."* It was so

kind of her to think of me during this first holiday season without Tim.

Bill and I were taking a walk in the park when grief overtook me and I burst into uncontrollable sobs. The grief comes in waves—less often now, but it still ebbs and flows. The holidays were especially difficult, that first Christmas without my son, with no hope of his return. One thing I know: There will be pangs of grief forever. I won't "get over it." I know now that he will always be a part of me. We were connected. The wiring just went bad, and he forgot all who loved him. There truly was nothing I could do to help him. He was a grown man, with his rights to privacy and his own choices. After numerous threats and failed attempts, he finally let himself depart this life. It was his decision, shaped by genetics and illness.

He was loving, talented, and lost. A boy needs a father's steady influence as he grows into manhood, and Tim was denied that. It was not his fault. I forgive him for the eleven years of silence when he cut me off. I learned to love him from a distance. But will I ever fully forgive myself for bringing a child into a chaotic, combative marriage? Perhaps not. No wonder he sometimes said he hadn't wanted to be born; in some way, he sensed the turbulence even from the womb. But such thoughts are futile now. What remains is love—deep, abiding love and compassion for his suffering. He will always be with me. He will always be in my heart.

Day 229
It is Sunday, March 9. I am beginning to feel a little calmer, a little more accepting with each day. Then, as I opened my checkbook for tax purposes, out fell a check I had written to retain a private investigator in Boston—a check I had never mailed. I had considered hiring him to do a wellness check on Tim last May, two months before he died. After much anguish, I decided it was too intrusive. I forgot about it—until today. Now the memory floods back. *What if I had sent it? Would it have changed the outcome? Would it have helped him? Or would I now feel responsible for provoking his final act?* Another sleepless night. I suspect these questions will never fully leave me, though perhaps they will visit less often.

My years of Catholic school and religious upbringing led me to believe in an afterlife. The only way I can endure this loss is to imagine that Tim is finally free of pain and anguish, that his soul has gone home. I try to picture him being greeted with love—by his grandmother, perhaps offering her homemade fudge brownies; by his favorite aunt and uncle, who predeceased him; and by many other relatives who adored him. This image brings me comfort: he is no longer alone, but embraced by love on the other side.

Day 313
Today is June 1—Tim's birthday. He would have been fifty-six years old. It has been 313 days since we lost him on July 23, 2024, and I have felt his absence—and his presence.

In the beginning, each day was unbearable, raw with pain so intense I could not imagine ever moving beyond it. Over time, I came to understand that I will never fully "recover." But I can learn to live with my grief. There are still moments, events, and anniversaries that bring waves of sorrow. Yet there are also moments of gratitude: for the love and laughter, the warmth and joy, and the many memories we shared. That is where I now place my focus.

This is not the ending I once imagined, but it is the life I have lived. I share my story so that it may offer strength to those walking a similar path and provide a measure of healing where there is pain. I am deeply grateful for the friends and companions who have guided me toward peace and renewal. May these words inspire others to find courage, to carry their love forward, and to embrace life again.

On the day I lost my son, he did not lose his mother. I will always be Timothy's mother. And he will always be with me.

SUICIDE

Research consistently shows that adolescents in single-parent or father-absent households face significantly higher risks of suicide and psychological disorders compared to peers in intact families. Studies indicate that three out of four teenage suicides occur in homes where a parent is absent, and fatherless children are particularly vulnerable. Additionally, composite measures of family structure, including divorce rates and the prevalence of female-headed households, strongly predict suicide risk among young adult and adolescent males. These findings highlight the profound impact of family stability on youth mental health—an impact I witnessed firsthand in my own life and in the loss of my son. Understanding these risks deepens the conversation about prevention, support, and the urgent need for compassion and awareness for families navigating these challenges.

Youth Suicide and Divorce — Single-Parent Homes

1. **Increased Risk in Single-Parent Families**
   "In a study of 146 adolescent friends of 26 adolescent suicide victims, teens living in

single-parent families are not only more likely to commit suicide but also more likely to suffer from psychological disorders, when compared to teens living in intact families."
Source: David A. Brent, et al., *Post-traumatic Stress Disorders in Peers of Adolescent Suicide Victims: Predisposing Factors and Phenomenology, Journal of the American Academy of Child and Adolescent Psychiatry*, 34 (1995): 209-215.

2. Fatherless Children at Greater Risk

"Fatherless children are at dramatically greater risk of suicide."
Source: U.S. Department of Health and Human Services, National Center for Health Statistics, Survey on Child Health, Washington, D.C., 1993.

3. Parental Absence and Teenage Suicide

"Three out of four teenage suicides occur in households where a parent has been absent."
Source: Jean Beth Eshtain, *Family Matters: The Plight of America's Children, The Christian Century*, July 1993, 14-21.

4. Family Structure Index as a Predictor

"A family structure index—a composite index based on the annual rate of children involved in divorce and the percentage of families with children present that are female-headed—is a strong predictor of suicide among young adult and adolescent white males."

Source: Patricia L. McCall and Kenneth C. Land, *Trends in White Male Adolescent, Young-Adult, and Elderly Suicide: Are There Common Underlying Structural Factors?*, *Social Science Research*, 23 (1994): 57-81.

Resources for Suicide Loss Survivors

Grieving a loved one lost to suicide is a journey no one should face alone. The resources below provide comfort, connection, and inspiration, offering meaningful ways to remember and celebrate their life while finding strength to move forward.

Alliance of Hope for Suicide Loss Survivors
allianceofhope.org

Created by survivors for survivors, this nonprofit provides online support, resources, and a 24/7 forum for those coping with the loss of a loved one to suicide.

National Suicide Prevention Lifeline
Call: 1-800-273-TALK (8255) | **Text:** START to 741741 | **Call/Text/Chat:** 988

Trained counselors are available 24/7 to listen, support, and connect you with resources.

CaringBridge
caringbridge.org

A free nonprofit platform supporting families during health journeys.

Ways to Honor a Loved One:

- Keep something of theirs with you.
- Support a cause or nonprofit meaningful to them.
- Create a scholarship or tribute donation.
- Plant a tree, garden, or other living memorial.
- Dedicate an event or start a new tradition in their memory.
- Share stories and photos to keep their memory alive.

These resources offer support, guidance, and inspiration for anyone navigating grief, helping keep the memory of a loved one alive while finding strength to move forward.

About the Author

Susan Kelley is a versatile and accomplished author, best known for her engaging explorations of relationships, life transitions, and personal resilience. Her work spans bestselling relationship guides and deeply personal memoirs, blending humor, honesty, and heartfelt insight.

She is the author of seven nonfiction books: *Real Women Send Flowers*, *Why Men Commit*, *Why Men Stray / Why Men Stay*, *The Second Time Around: Everything You Need to Know to Make Your Remarriage Happy*, *I Oprahed and Other Adventures of a Woman of a Certain Age*, *Forever Florence: A Memoir*, and most recently *The Diagnosis Diaries* (2023). Her best-selling relationship books have been translated into several languages, including Japanese, Polish, Turkish, and Dutch.

Susan has appeared as a guest relationship expert on *The Oprah Winfrey Show*, *The Early Show* on CBS News, MSNBC, Fox TV, and numerous other national and local programs, as well as hundreds of radio interviews across the United States and Canada.